ADVANCE PRAISE

"Managers and leaders need to understand the importance of these human relations or human processes ... they need to establish them, facilitate them and continuously develop them to achieve truly outstanding and sustainable results. This impressive book, *The Heartbeat of Excellence*, will be helpful for many emerging leaders and teams to achieve sustainable high performance for their organizations in an ever-changing world."

Detlef Krost, Chief Technical Officer, Nestlé USA

"By applying this human process based on our Swiss democratic values of trust, tolerance and humility, I was able to make the difference as a leader and enable my team to emerge fully autonomous and become sustainably high-performing."

Chris Ayer, Head of Operations Coffee and Beverages in Europe, the Middle East and North Africa, Nestlé

Published by
LID Publishing Limited
The Record Hall, Studio 204,
16-16a Baldwins Gardens,
London EC1N 7RJ, UK

info@lidpublishing.com
www.lidpublishing.com

A member of:

BPR ⊛
businesspublishersroundtable.com

© Curt Blattner, 2020
© LID Publishing Limited, 2020

Printed in Latvia by Jelgavas Tipogrāfija
ISBN: 978-1-912555-69-7

Cover and page design: Caroline Li

Curt Blattner

THE **HEARTBEAT** OF **EXCELLENCE**

The Design of
Changing Sustainably,
the Swiss Way ✚

MADRID | MEXICO CITY | LONDON
NEW YORK | BUENOS AIRES
BOGOTA | SHANGHAI | NEW DELHI

CONTENTS

PREFACE

I live in a country where a cow is queen and a wrestler king. The Eringer Breeder's Association supports the yearly competition of the Swiss cow fights, an event visited by thousands of spectators, professionals and fans and followed by many more on live television across the country. The owners and their families make sure that their sturdy, stocky animals, like pets, are well looked after and cared for. Two cows challenge each other to a fight, manifesting their natural instinct to determine who should lead the herd. They clash head on and shove each other in turns through the sand of the arena, their snouts close to the ground, neck muscles bulging and tails held high, and when they use their horns, one is reminded of combat as witnessed in Olympic Fencing. As soon as one animal feels inferior, it abandons the fight, and the encounter is over. The cow winning the final is declared queen for the year.

The king is a human wrestler, crowned every three years with a wreath made out of oak leaves. The event, organized by the Schwinger Association of Switzerland, gathers the best wrestlers in the country, all avocational (they earn their living otherwise), to compete in front of over 50,000 onlookers in a temporary stadium specially erected for the occasion and is nationally televised. It is a tough but fair sport, characterized by a mix of extreme bodily and mental human strength, cunning tactics and the dream of glory. Despite their fierce encounters, the competitors fight fair and are respectful of one another. It is custom to shake hands before and for the winner to wipe off the sawdust from the adversary's back after each fight.

These two national events, full of rituals and traditions, represent the Swiss way, where the values of fairness and respect prevail for all the principal actors and the audience alike. They are figureheads of the thousands of national associations that infiltrate the socio-economic landscape of Switzerland at all levels. They are also examples of successful organizations where members take responsibility, are empowered and in cooperation, and where trust and honesty in human relationships are important for reaching their goals.

This insight has been the initiator to address the one common denominator as the foundation and basic condition in any organization's journey to excellence: human relations. It is there where the heartbeat of excellence lies and the creation of high-performing human relations in an organization is the red thread of this book. In *The Heartbeat of Excellence: The Design of Changing Sustainably, the Swiss Way*, we describe how this happens. The key element of this process is emergence: the genesis of high-performing human relations arising from the dynamics of a team acting as one entity, as a single body, and the leader enabling co-creation. These dynamics are known and have been described in literature before. However, the combination of these forces, their integration into one approach and their application are novel and give leadership and self-organizing teams a new and unprecedented spin. The uniqueness of the concept lies in accelerating an organization's journey to excellence by managing high-performing human relations sustainably, in a human process, accessible to all, using the three contracts of the Emerging Change Model: vision, mission and cooperation (Laugeri, 2015). The model is easily useable. It is presented in Chapter 8 and explained with practical examples from business. We use Switzerland and the way its people live its direct democracy as an illustration of how the concept of emergence is applied in a big organization, and we call it the Swiss way of changing sustainably. My intention is in no way to describe in detail the theoretical aspects of the model. I refer the reader to Madeleine Laugeri's own publications.

The workings of Swiss democracy with its values of trust, tolerance, fairness and humbleness have influenced the way I approach work and, perhaps even more critically, the way I understand leadership styles and organization structures. In business, I have seen how people working together successfully for a common cause yields a competitive advantage, but I have also seen teams fail. I had a hunch that there was a unifying element missing when teams in organizations did not succeed in their cooperation and, since the beginning of my professional career, I have been driven by the quest to identify what that is. It is the human process of emergence. My adventures in business, while bearing different responsibilities in different countries, have shown me the force a team generates when it fully emerges.

It took me a long time, however, to discover what catalyses emergence and how it influences performance.

Switzerland is small, is a prospering country and is recognized for its social advancements, individual freedom and well-proven democracy. They are the results of its history, where changing sustainably was enabled by the emergence of its people over centuries. Emergence and its inherent values are deeply embedded in Switzerland's socio-economic tissue and are instrumental in how the country's heart beats for excellence, from the world titles of its sports champions – the queen and king crowned by national associations – to the successes of its institutions and corporations.

It peaks in the way the country, comprising 0.1% of the world's population, is governed. The top executive power of the Swiss Confederation, the Federal Council, is a team of seven councillors and they are all equally responsible for the management of the council's operations, strategy and decisions. Because there is no single authority in charge, they can address conflicts between peers, and work in autonomy and cooperation for their solutions to emerge from consensus. Exchange and confrontation between the council members are tough, but the quality of their relations allows for cooperation and constructive dialogue in all humbleness and fairness, attributes that impress the normal citizen every now and then. You might easily cross a federal councillor at the train station, on the way home or during your holidays on the ski run. There is no need of bodyguards, and they are liable to greet you when you make eye contact, or even enter into conversation should you adapt to their speed of cross-country skiing.

When visiting Bern and coincidently passing by the government buildings, you might cast a glance through the ground-floor window and catch the president of the confederation feeding the copy machine.

Changing sustainably could seem contradictory to the famous breakthrough change mentality often advocated in current business. However, I believe that successful innovations, even the most unexpected, are the result of a sustainable long-term change process where emergence reigns and our best example is our own evolution. Research carried out by Michael Tomasello shows how the early behaviours in the ontogenesis of our species (e.g., the helping and cooperativeness of young human children), are not created by a socialization process, but rather by their natural tendency to sympathize. The behaviours of cooperation have their origin in our phylogeny; they are a product of and have emerged from our biological evolution, the universal, sustainable change process ruling our world. This insight could sound quite optimistic: a key driver of why and who we are is the process of changing sustainably with emergence.

Emerging change proved successful through all fields of business during my professional career and it has changed the lives of many on its way. As it turns out, the potential of applying emerging change is still huge and most organizations need to accelerate to avoid the circumstance where there's no second chance. Changing sustainably – the Swiss way – is beneficial to anyone interested in the journey to excellence.

A PARADIGM SHIFT IN THE JOURNEY TO EXCELLENCE

"Continuous improvement is better than delayed perfection."

Mark Twain

The president of Sunset Scavengers, a garbage collection firm, sits behind his desk, smiling into the camera. A gold chain hangs from his wrist, reflecting the sunlight entering from the window, as he picks up a miniature garbage truck. He leans forward and exclaims with a drawl: "I love garbage." How can you love garbage, and why would you? This is the remaining image of my first encounter with *In Search of Excellence* (Tom Peters and Robert H. Waterman, 2004). *In Search of Excellence* (first published in 1982) and later *A Passion for Excellence* (Tom Peters and Nancy Austin, 1985) had an enormous effect on the development of leadership for successful businesses ever since, with its stories of leaders and companies passionately doing the unexpected and extraordinary and being highly successful. They caused emotions in crowds of people. When asked about the book, Tom Peters said, "I had no idea what I was doing when I wrote *Search*. There was no carefully designed work plan. There was no theory that I was out to prove."

There was suddenly an entirely different attitude toward management and leadership. It appeared there was no contradiction anymore between having fun and still being highly successful in business. For me, a young engineer employed in North America during the time, this was a game changer. I had thought work had to be serious, rational and analytical, nothing else. In my short career, I had witnessed the very limited leadership style of command and control, and suddenly I was confronted with alternatives. We had been trained to receive and give orders and reach goals in a disciplined, standardized and structured way, and my experience in the army had only reinforced that. Conveying a vision, expressing a clear mission and communicating to the people had always been crucial for good management, but expressing emotion and passion were not considered positive attributes in decision-making.

With *In Search of Excellence* and *A Passion for Excellence*, the potential for management became radically different. Leaders were now to be inspiring. They should show emotions in public and advocate for their employees' autonomy. Individuals were expected to take responsibility, to think and act out of the box. It was a total paradigm shift. Work environments began to change, setting the stage for my following professional life.

In *In Search for Excellence*, Peters outlines the 'eight common attributes of excellence'. But I remember that what touched me most was the mindset of "It all comes from people". The authors call for employee involvement, engagement of the front line in productivity improvements, employees as the source of knowledge and quality improvement, supported through flat organizations. People could become autonomous, which would help them individually make change happen. Each person is of value. Perhaps this all sounds like common sense, but it had definitely not been evident in the rational, technocratic and patronizing business world I had witnessed up until then.

The awareness of people-centred management and leadership in business soon turned into a mass movement. It was timely, as the reality of the limitations of existing economic behaviour in the 1970s became obvious to the broad public, and people were receptive to a new purpose, rooted already in the political and social turmoil of the late 1960s. The establishment needed to change, and power rearranged. Business thinking, models and systems for continuous improvement and the idea of moving toward excellence was readily adopted in this context. Management gurus (e.g., William Edwards Deming, Peter Drucker or other leaders such as Konosuke Matsushita or Taiichi Ono), shared well-developed and powerful change processes. These concepts became famous and popular in numerous books, publications, case studies and management schools; it was fashionable to talk 'CI' (Continuous Improvement), 'LEAN Manufacturing', 'Just in Time', 'Kanban', 'Total Quality' or 'Kai-Zen'. There was a flood of options for businesses, CEOs and managers to pick from and heydays for consultants who knew exactly what to apply when for successful change. Industry and business quickly accepted; they needed to increase productivity in an accelerated way with the rise of the electronic industry. The notions of management commitment, of empowering and enabling people and organizations to develop to new heights, were everywhere. Organizations were ready to change and to consider management giving purpose and autonomy to their employees, and they were doing it. How effective was this and how was this now supposed to be done correctly?

Apart from power to the people, from their proclaimed individual liberty and rights, there was another element that was surprising in this new paradigm. Suddenly there were business managers being very successful with people-centred management by addressing the importance of emotions at work and promoting sound human relations in their organizations. Many of these companies showed excellent business results and became leaders for continuous improvement. Their CEOs, highly honoured for their achievements, started to write books about their journeys to excellence. In these stories, successful leadership was very much related to the attributes of the leader. The good managers were good in reasoning and convincing by addressing the hard and the soft side of management, and they seemed to do it naturally. Yet it appeared there was little awareness of how we *all* could benefit from managing the soft side in a structured way. As it says in *In Search of Excellence*, "Professionalism is equated with hard-headed rationality. It seeks detached, analytical justification for all decisions" (T. Peters and R.H. Waterman, 2004). Despite the quest for more emotions in management, rational reasoning predominated professionally. It seemed as if most of the individual leaders in business still were making their decisions based on the analysis of reports, figures and statistics. Emotions were fine in theory, but running a business was still something else.

I grew up and completed my education in a democratic society, an essential circumstance in my desire to adopt people-centred leadership in business management. The new business paradigm of mobilizing the power of all employees in co-constructing a fruitful future of a company made sense. In spite of my initial surprise, it struck me, consciously or not, as normal.

Today I would relate my reaction then to the spirit of liberty and collaboration I had seen in Switzerland's direct democracy. To me, this spirit is in contrast to the mighty and powerful authorities of any organization that force decisions from the top down. Management should be centred around people. It's common sense. What is, then, the big deal? Well, it should be more than lip service. People need to have the free space and simultaneously the permission and protection to take responsibility as individuals and as groups. They must be fully involved in value creation for the benefit of the whole, through helping each other. Swiss democracy is said to be rooted in this spirit of freedom, where the people have cooperated in managing their private and public affairs as far back as the 13th century.

Surprisingly, we encounter in the latest management books the words 'freeing up' or 'liberation'. Some of the most fashionable management talks in Europe nowadays are about 'l'entreprise libérée' (the liberated enterprise). It seems there is a need to liberate a company, a business, from something that is hindering excellence. In such a context, the paradigm shift the business world experienced in the early 1980s and thereon would feel quite logical. The wish for people to be free in thought, speech and act is deeply embedded in humanity and the realization of this feat was and still is a continuous struggle, as history and present times tell us.

It is worthwhile to explain how the spirit of liberty and liberation is seen to have evolved over the centuries in Switzerland, and what role it played in the past and continues to play today. It is very likely that the workings of Switzerland's direct democracy and the Swiss way of changing sustainably, through autonomy and emergence, is at the origin of the prosperity and peace in our country. And this can serve as a prime example of how people's hearts can beat for excellence in any organization.

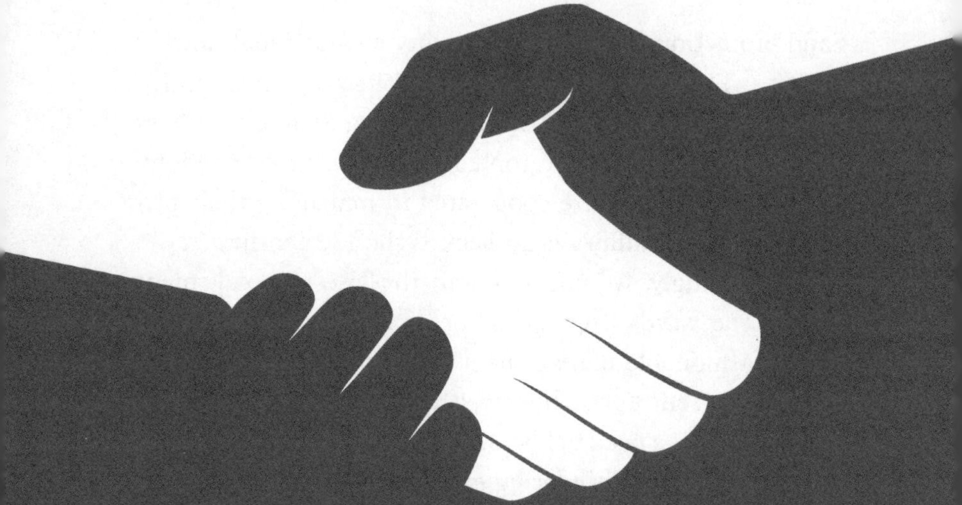

2

THE
SWISS
WAY

"Prosperity is the
best protector
of principle."

Mark Twain

Democratic structures are, by definition, people-centred; however, this is not necessarily true to the same extent for all democracies. The belief in the autonomous individual or groups and the principle of subsidiarity are fundamental and anchored in the Swiss democratic system. All citizens have a direct, active role to play and responsibilities to take in the decisions regarding the future of the country. Our current regime in Switzerland is a result of continuous improvement over many centuries. Thomas Maissen explains in *Schweizer Heldengeschichten* (*Swiss Heroic Stories*) about the evolution of the Swiss Confederation up to the federalist and national state of today. In his book, he refers to the well-known events in Swiss history that have supposedly shaped the character of the country but also questions some of those famous stories of Swiss heroes and their followers. The legend of Wilhelm Tell is a tale of a rightful citizen in the 13th century fighting for freedom and independence. He is said to have openly opposed the injustices imposed on the people, shot an arrow into an apple placed on his kid's head and rid the country of the tyrant responsible with his famous crossbow. (The latter having become the hallmark of Swiss quality on export products across the globe today.) While there is no historically validated documentation of Tell's existence, despite the many stories transmitted over the centuries of his heroic deeds, it is the wonderful drama by Friedrich Schiller that has moved our minds and hearts. The apple shot, however, exists already in earlier legends, e.g., in Scandinavian history such a task, performed by Toko, the Viking, as the hero, is mentioned and widely recognized, and there is the probability that Tell's story is a copy (as my friend would say: *"Si non è vero, è ben' trovato"*). But even if the reality of the living Tell might seem doubtful, the spirit of fighting for freedom and people's rights, which, as historians confirm, was probably present in the 13th century in said region, is well represented in the character. Was Tell the hunter out of the mountains, the upright citizen or the rebel? Was he a single person or did he exist at all? Historians have different opinions. What they mostly agree on is the likelihood of several similar conflicts and events at the time, as described in the hero's story. The cities and valleys in the Middle Ages, in the areas and regions of what we call Central Switzerland today, had been cooperating and consulting already for a common purpose during the period of Tell's presumed existence, and cohesion of the population and the wish for maintaining autonomy could very well have influenced the outcomes of the disputes then and the political movements thereafter.

Famine, plague and poverty were ubiquitous in those days, and life often remained tough and miserable. But there were also periods and regions where the 'demos' were already living satisfactorily well: the lands delivered, trade was good and the king far away – maintaining economic prosperity and political and social rights and security in such an environment was priority. The 'demos' of the Middle Ages consisted of the leaders of status who held the economic and political powers, and they were a minority in the population. The people with no rights, e.g., serfs, women, children and the poor, were excluded (achieving coherence for all is a continuous battle: the last canton in Switzerland to introduce women's right to vote was forced to do so by a ruling of the federal court in 1990). Still, in the early 19th century, the federalists and founding fathers of the US constitution claimed that the Swiss system was meant to guarantee the power to the rich and mighty. The direct democracy of Switzerland was, in their eyes, nothing more than a system to maximize earnings of the wealthy and the parties supporting them and, in spite of their close and common democratic spirit, they refused to take the Swiss Confederation of the time as a model for their plans.

Later, it was the US constitution that served as the blueprint for Switzerland and its present federalist structure. In this process, the individual states, the cantons, which today collaborate on a superior level in the confederation, the 'Confoederatio Helveticorum' (CH), kept a large part of the political power. (Cantons are political structures that have their own constitutions and legislative and executive authorities. They have a single chamber parliament and govern the areas including schooling, the tax system, the police force and construction control.) Political progress at the time was laborious and rich in conflicts; it was a tug-of-war between the liberal centralists, mainly the big cities, and the conservative Catholic cantons. This hostility within the confederation was a struggle that lasted over centuries and led to several confrontations on the battlefield. However, fighting ended in 1847, and the first Swiss Constitution followed a year later. After nearly another 50 years, liberal nationalists and conservative federalists agreed to cooperate, a milestone in forming the base of our modern direct democracy in Switzerland. The outcomes included revisions of the constitution and the installation of the people's political tools and procedures for emerging on a federal level – the 'people's initiative' and 'people's referendum'. The *referendum* is the demand for a vote on a decision of parliament before it is put into effect. Any Swiss citizen can start a referendum: 50,000 signatures of persons with the right to vote must be collected and presented to the Federal Office within 100 days. The *people's initiative* is the call for a vote on a proposal to change or modify the constitution. It can be initiated by any Swiss citizen, requires 100,000 signatures and has to be signed off by the Federal Office within 18 months.

A federal structure implies decentralized power and autonomy, and this is deeply engraved in Swiss society today. The extent of this is shown in the examples of our four national languages and our many dialects, which are each unique to a canton or sometimes even a valley. Approximately two thirds of the Swiss speak a specific dialect of Swiss German (there are 26 cantons, of which Swiss German is spoken in 21). Children will speak the dialect of their canton even if they live only a short distance off the border to the neighbour; one can easily identify where a person comes from by his dialect, but not by his languages. Three of the four national languages taught in school (German, French and Italian) will cross the borders of the cantons, and there are four cantons which are officially bilingual. The fourth language is Rumantsch-Ladin, spoken by a minority in five variations; it is the main language in the first years of school in the valleys of the canton Graubünden.

Dialects are sedentary, having developed from the inside, the living evidence of the conditions and circumstances that led to Switzerland's federal structure with its decentralized autonomy and cooperation. Languages, however, infiltrated from the outside, transported by different conquerors, from the Roman Empire to Karl the Great and later through the soft and silent colonization of the Alemanni in the space between Bodensee (Lake Constance),

Lac Léman (Lake Geneva), the River Rhine in the North and the southern plains beyond the Alps. "The Swiss nation of today is a collective and unified political structure of several languages and several different cultures, where living together in mutual respect stands above unification, in contrast to a nation of single race of common blood, territory and language" (Bergier, 1988).

In early times, the families who settled in isolated regions were forced to take matters into their own hands and help each other for survival; they were in charge of their own destiny in their valleys and villages because, simply put, there was nobody around to question it. The topography, the rugged mountains, the remote high valleys, the rivers and lakes hindered easy access, interference and meddling by strangers and foreign rulers. The sparse habitat of these original settlers was just not attractive enough for invaders and intruders; there was too small a profit to make for the size of the effort. Families grew into clans and communities, autonomously governing the areas they occupied, the 'pagi' (place/land, in Latin), and often benefiting from privileges granted by the emperor or his loyal vassals. Belonging to such an autonomous group of people was hereditary. Descendants belonged automatically to their family's place of origin, and it still holds true for Swiss citizenship today. The township, the smallest autonomous political unit, attributes citizenship based on one's bloodline, independent of where a person was born (filling in 'place of birth' as requested in foreign forms makes no sense to Swiss citizens) and applications for Swiss citizenship are presented to the town council.

When asking a Swiss where he is from, he will answer with the name of his canton of origin and sometimes even his township. Traditional Swiss are proud of their roots and moving house was and still is not the norm. Evenings and mornings, public transportation and highways are crammed with commuters travelling to work for the day or the week from their hometown somewhere in the valleys or hills to the city.

The decentralized power and autonomy in the 'pagi' led to the emergence of decentralized cooperation between them. This was supported by a dynamic network of alliances in the early days of the confederation and is guaranteed by the Swiss Constitution in current times. The classic dichotomy of a federalist structure is ensuring decentralized autonomy in the cantons and townships, e.g., the appreciation and usage of the dialects and the recognition of the four official national languages in our educational systems versus confederating for common purposes and interests on a national level as, for example, in the system of financial compensation between cantons. The workings of this balance are difficult to grasp: the townships and the cantons collect the main taxes and decide on big issues like construction of schools and hospitals or refugee integration. Operating in equilibrium and achieving a common national strategy on such sensitive subjects, specifically toward the outside world, needs continuous constructive dialoguing and finding consensus in the frame of the Swiss values of tolerance, trust and humbleness. It is worthwhile mentioning two special events that shaped Swiss history and are often linked to the roots of Swiss direct democracy and its underlying values and beliefs: the 'Landsgemeinden' and the 'Bundesbrief'.

Swiss traditionalists and populists willingly mention the 'Landsgemeinden' as the origin of political autonomy and empowerment in our democracy. In the Middle Ages, they were, and in two instances still are, a form of exerting democratic rights in the cantons. Rightful citizens, the sovereign, gather in the central plaza, an open space of the capital, to promote their political agenda. They have the right to speak and vote, the latter done by raising (or not) their hand for a yes or no. All cantons abandoned this way of parliament on their route to our modern federal structure, with the exception of Appenzell Innerrhoden and Glarus, and those are worth seeing. It is a common belief that our direct democracy derived straight from the 'Landsgemeinden'. Its practices of open exchange and dialogue in public for finding consensus and making decisions have become rituals in Swiss politics and the prime grounds for emergence to flourish upon. They have inspired citizens to embed their cooperation in an autonomous way.

Current Swiss populistic parties use the image of the 'Landsgemeinden' as propaganda. This requires a call for caution. They refer to the 'old' autonomy and freedom of the tribes and families in the Middle Ages, as the sole and irrefutable needs of modern direct democracy, to argue against all new intentions for Switzerland's future, e.g., the integration in Europe. Unfortunately, this can be misleading. One is prone to bend the facts of the historic circumstances for gaining a political advantage today: the constellation of political and social power at the time did not allow the whole population to speak up freely in public, a fact often forgotten today. Individual freedom for all was not on the agenda then. Limitless admiration of the values inherent in the 'Landsgemeinden' may lead to overrating their significance for democratic requirements of today.

It may evoke the risk of omitting the inglorious fact that the rights of the major part of the population centuries ago were bluntly oppressed by the mighty. It was a common global reality then (and in many parts of our world still is today) and is the reason why, in our modern times, such dogmatic comparisons turn out to be questionable.

Another famous milestone in the development of Swiss democracy is the 'Bundesbrief', the Federal Charter of Alliance. This charter was issued and originally signed and sealed by the leaders of the townships and the valleys of the three areas known as Uri, Schwyz and Nidwalden – and dated beginning of August 1291. It is the oldest available document of an alliance in Swiss history and describes the agreements between these regions to help and stand by each other for ensuring their internal order and external security. Now, alliances were a common form for states to support each other against external risks and danger during the Middle Ages (Maissen, 2015). At the time the 'Bundesbrief' was signed, the death of the ruling king, Rudolf von Habsburg, had caused a void in the kingdom, which included the areas in central Switzerland. For the locals this meant risking new, disadvantageous or detrimental laws or dominance by a new, unwelcome ruler. The peril of losing their control over the Gotthard pass, the major route for goods, people and livestock through the Alps, was to be taken seriously. In such political and socio-economic uncertainty, the alliance clearly made sense (Bergier, 1988). There seems, however, to be a common understanding by historians that this alliance was neither intended for claiming independence nor starting a revolution. Although it was a declaration for maintaining the given rights of the regions and ensuring cooperation between the existing parties, it clearly also had the character of preserving the freedom and power of the ruling families, granted by external authorities and forces, while ensuring the obligations of the subjects. However, this is not what Swiss patriots want to have understood today. They see the events around 1291 and the alliance thereof as the birth of Swiss independence and a sign of uprising against external powers. This interpretation has endured over time, in some instances even inspiring insurrection, such as the French Revolution. Regardless of whether one sees the Bundesbrief as an alliance protecting the status quo or an early instance of revolutionary action, it is certainly an example of how cooperation and consensus, together with the control mechanisms the different parties established, agreed and adhered to, have become the driving forces for the creation of the Swiss way.

Cooperation, consensus and mutual control likely played a prominent role in the progress and the continuous developments of the political and social structures in Swiss history; at least they seem to fit perfectly into the picture conveyed by the documents available and the narrated traditions and events. As such, the courts of arbitration (Bergier, 1988) are essential instruments to address internal conflicts of individuals and groups in public. They had proven effective then and are still fundamental for consensus building. These drivers for changing sustainably emerged as a consequence of the autonomy, the trust in human relations and the strength and quality of the people's bonds and evolved, over the centuries, to the cornerstones of our democracy today. They are prerequisites for the prosperity and peace of modern Switzerland. Benefiting sustainably, however, from these conditions and circumstances requires the engagement and the emergence of all citizens. At present, Switzerland has 25% foreign residents (persons without Swiss citizenship). They do not have the right to vote on federal issues, and it remains to be seen how this will be managed and how it will influence our democratic development in the future. We cannot disregard this huge segment of the population in the emergence for coherence and for changing sustainably.

Involving everybody in a group or organization and supporting the exchange of a multitude of different opinions is essential for emergence and relevant for cooperation. Permission and protection for unrestricted interaction and alignment of those involved must be guaranteed; an organization must establish space and resources for ensuring sufficient opportunities for exchange. This is applied in the whole of Swiss society, from its innumerous associations and small enterprises, its 2,222 townships (as of 1 January 2018) and their communities, to the way the country is led. The executive power in the political structure of Switzerland lies in the hands of a team of councillors of equal status: five or seven for the cantons and seven for the confederation, so the power of the parts is in balance with the power of the whole.

Being a member of the Swiss legislature is a part-time job. Members of federal as well as cantonal parliament earn their living as employees, employers or entrepreneurs in business and institutes of public or private nature; a social cross section from schools to banks, artisanal and small companies to corporations, farmers, unions and NGOs is represented in parliament in person. In Switzerland you know and relate to your representative in the canton or maybe even on the federal level. Diversity is assured and anonymity excluded and, when things go wrong, for no system is perfect, control and correction can be made on the highest level by the citizens and their elected representatives. How else would it be possible in the 21st century, under the pressure of the public, to vote out a councillor in federal executive government against his will and the will of his party? The highest executive power of the nation lies with a team of multiparty structure, the Federal Council. Federal councillors are elected in such a way that the four biggest political parties are represented, the magic formula. Their decisions are made in cooperation and with consensus (collegial principle) and stand above the opinions and the slogans of the different political parties. The Federal Council communicates and supports their statements to the outside as one voice; there is no single, exceptional leader responsible. However, for practical reasons, there is the need of a single representative towards other nations who is called president of the confederation. He or she is determined by parliament every year and is not the head of state but the official representative of Switzerland when required; the federal councillors each take turns, a custom respected during election. The president's leadership authority in the team, as *primus inter pares*, is limited to chairing the council's meetings and to the casting vote in the Federal Council, in case a vote must be taken and a majority not reached. The seven councillors are the heads of the seven federal departments. Each member is accountable for her or his departmental areas of activities and for the exchange of their own strategic elements in the team, the Federal Council, to cover their needs. They are all equally responsible for the management of the council's operations and strategy and because there is no single authority in charge, conflicts can openly be addressed.

The basics of these principles permeate through the political landscape all the way down to the townships and into the innumerable amount of associations and cooperatives making up the social tissue of Switzerland. Some aspire to participate in their township's councils and others with a common motivation of all kinds – music, sports, agriculture and many more – convene regularly and cooperate toward common goals in their associations. The country is known for its laws of easily forming an association and soliciting membership. Having one or several memberships somewhere in a club is fundamental to Swiss society and the resulting web of these groups in Switzerland makes interaction easy and comprehensive for all, yielding autonomy and cooperation as a fact of daily life. Eventually it spills over into the political awareness of the public and the important socio-economical layer of small and midsized enterprises. Finally, it does not halt at the doors of Swiss national institutions or international corporations.

Another consequence of our democratic structure is the schooling and apprenticeship system. Private schools are for expatriates and diplomats, elite thinking is frowned upon and proper education is open to all in a decentralized way. And still the two Swiss Federal Institutes of Technology are ranked among the top, ETH-Z in 3rd and EPF-L in 11th place in the global league of Technical Universities (QS Top Universities, 2019).

Changing sustainably the Swiss way covers :
- Emotions and rationality as equal partners. Expressing the values of respect and humbleness in open exchanges, as well as sincere emotions, is key to the innumerous

groups of sports, industry and associations and blends fully into the democratic life of the country (Chapter 3)

- Human relations and coherence. The executive powers of the Swiss political landscape act with one voice, thanks to their high-performing human relations. It is the part of the Swiss way that is described in the cooperation contract of emerging change, and allows for aligning with the objectives of government as one entity and ensures coherence in the country (Chapter 4)
- Autonomous cooperation. It is the force that aims for interdependency and is anchored in the values of trust, tolerance, fairness and individual freedom in the Swiss population (Chapter 5)
- Planned change. It is the dynamic of the leader managed by the mission contract of Emerging Change in a constructive dialogue with the group. Excessive planned change kills trust and tolerance. People will have difficulties initiating emergence and the organization will stall on its journey to excellence. The Swiss way of changing sustainably offers a remedy that is applicable even at the level of the Federal Council (Chapter 6)
- A human process with emerging change. Technical and knowledge management processes are in balance with the human process in the Swiss way of changing sustainably, which renders the journey to excellence efficient as shown in the Swiss apprenticeship system (Chapter 7)

3

PEOPLE: EMOTIONS AND RATIONALITY

"Every emotion,
if sincere,
is involuntary."

Mark Twain

Roger Federer stands in the middle of the court surrounded by officials, referees, ball-boys and ball-girls and in front of tens of thousands of spectators in the tennis arena and millions on television. He just won, again, the Australian Open, one of the four Grand Slams of the ITF (International Tennis Federation). He lifts the winner's cup above his head and the crowd roars. His face glows and, in spite of being exhausted after the enormous task he has just achieved, he still smiles. He has all reason to. The presenter passes him the microphone and everybody is ready for him to explain what he went through in the match. He first thanks the spectators, then the officials and all others who are present or had supported him. He directs friendly and supportive words to his adversary, standing by and, of course, he never forgets to specially mention his family and his team. Then something happens, which probably many of us are waiting for. Suddenly he has difficulty continuing to speak and his eyes turn wet. He lowers his gaze, has to pause for a moment and use his wristband to wipe his tears. A few seconds later, he again faces the audience and continues, with a slight curve on his lips and eyes still shiny. This sequence of emotions might repeat itself during his appearance.

Roger is liked by millions of people. Many adore him; he is undoubtedly a world star and a leader. I believe there are only very few people who know about Roger and would not wish to have dinner with him, take advice from him, certainly if you are a tennis player, or even just talk to him. Why is this? He is a master of his trade, if not *the* master. It's unbelievable what he has achieved in his field of professional activity and beyond over so many years. But best of all,

Roger comes across to us as truly emotional; simply put, as a human being. The combination of technical superiority, rationally explainable, with the expression of sincere feelings in all humbleness is extremely powerful and makes him a captivating person, a champion of bonding and a Swiss ambassador of excellence. Once we see him in this situation, even if only on television, we then cannot fail to sympathize with Roger and we decide we like him.

Technical superiority together with sincere emotional bonding is part of the Swiss way. So is emergence. The Swiss way of changing sustainably, the heartbeat of excellence, has shaped and moulded the country for centuries and stamped freedom and prosperity on its society. It is flabbergasting to see how Roger Federer piles up cup after title, delivering outstanding results; but others have done or are doing it too. When we, however, follow the way he plays and has played sustainably over more than two decades and how he managed to reach the level of fame he hovers at today, our hearts beat for Roger and excellence pops to our mind. This feeling is not only related to tennis but definitely to the person and what he represents. We just love to watch him on or off court. He says how incredibly fortunate he is to have met the right people at the right time in his career, how lucky he was on the way, although one could argue those decisions were his (Ubha & Macfarlane, 2019).

It is our sustained qualities as human beings, our intrinsic values, honest feelings and behaviours that create the space for and the quality of the human relationships around us. This allows for cooperation in all autonomy with our fellow men and women (family, friends, teams, coaches) and those unplanned situations in life to emerge for us to make the right decisions. Roger did make those decisions, maybe not alone; what counts in my story are the conditions, circumstances and constellations that permit any team to emerge and set the course for the path to excellence. The heartbeat of excellence is felt where true emotions emerge in trust, fairness, tolerance and humbleness and human relations become high performing. That is the process of changing sustainably, the Swiss way.

In our patriarchal society, rational thinking is masculine and emotions are feminine, so it is not surprising that the importance of emotions in business is largely underestimated. Leaders in our Western society are meant to make tough decisions, some on the spot. Leaders are depicted as always being in control, like fighter pilots; their leadership qualities are associated with what certain watchmakers insinuate in advertisements as the characteristics of real men. Big boys don't cry. Even the ladies at the helm of our companies today are often measured by leadership qualities related to this masculine image. In our Western society, it is unacceptable to think that women would lead differently and viewing the corporate world of an organization by gender is still inadmissible. Everybody must be treated equally, no question. Why, however, should we miss out on capitalizing on the variety of strengths in a group or organization?

In the past, we had heard, leaders were meant to be rational and to act in reason of an apparent logic and that emotions do not really have much space in leadership. But are the decisions a manager needs to take, irrelevant on which level, primarily a function of reasoning with rationality? Does reasoning solely by rationality guarantee better decisions and, as a consequence, better leadership? The answer seems to be no, and it looks as if the dualism of *cogito, ergo sum* is wrong, or maybe we have just misunderstood (Damasio, 2010).

As Antonio R. Damasio, celebrated neuroscientist and Head of the Brain and Creativity Institute at the University of Southern California, says: "First we are and then we think." He questions strongly the separation of body and spirit inherent in Descartes' philosophy: "We cannot separate how we think from who we are, e.g., how our brain is structured. Brain circuits are responsible for our spirit and emotions. They are genetically defined, modulated and structured by environment and experiences, and formed by the social and cultural context of the individual. They are constantly influencing our behaviour and decisions."

There is a structure behind the role of emotions and their relationship to reasoning in decision-making, and it appears to be just how our brain works; these are connections we all have independent of our culture and these structures confirm how important emotions are in how we make decisions.

The human brain has evolved from its very old and basic functionalities, the reptilian brain, to how the newest and latest discoveries, the cortex with the frontal lobes, operate. Dionysus, the ancient Greek god of wine, joy and ecstasy, represents our unconsciously working emotional world of lust, pleasure and desire, buried deep down in us, while Apollo, the ancient Greek god of purity, represents ethics and moderation, concepts that are emerging from the younger parts of our brain, the cerebral cortex. We must accept this and master the combination of the rational and the emotional brain in our decision-making processes.

Unmistakably, decisions are driven by the moral frame of a society, containing the conventions to which we all have agreed to adhere. As human beings, we have a genetically preset and a culturally defined understanding of what is acceptable and what is not. Although the rules and the conventions may be quite clear, our decisions on how to act within this framework might not. We are definitely not only rational when we make moral decisions as the rules would expect us to be, but surely also emotional.

In the trolley problem, Joshua Greene, renowned neuroscientist at Harvard, demonstrates how our emotional brain influences the outcome of a mental experiment. It is based on a well-known philosophical enigma established by Philippa Foot. There are two scenarios with similar set-ups. In the first scenario, you are the driver of a runaway trolley. The brakes have failed, and the trolley is approaching a fork in the track at top speed. If you do nothing, the train will stay left, where it will run over five people who are on the track. All five will die. If, however, you steer the train right – this involves flicking a switch and turning the wheel – you will swerve onto a track where there is one person. What do you do? Are you willing to intervene and change the path of the trolley? In this hypothetical case, people agree it is better to kill fewer people, so they turn the trolley. It is simple arithmetic. It is also the reason for the existence of our constitutional rights. They are made to stand above our moral thinking. Our cultural evolution and understanding will not allow such a decision for the reason of protection of life and dignity of every individual in our society independent of the situation. But then how should we decide? The dilemma is well-known and marvelously presented in the ARD film *Terror – Ihr Urteil* (*The Verdict*) after the stage play by Ferdinand von Schirach.

In the second scenario, you are standing on a footbridge over the trolley track. You see a trolley racing out of control, speeding toward five people who are on the track. All five will die unless the trolley can be stopped. Standing next to you on the footbridge is a very large man. He is leaning over the railing, watching the trolley run toward the men. If you sneak up on the man and give him a little push, he will fall over the railing and into the path of the trolley. Because he is so big, he will stop the trolley from killing the people on the track. Do you push the man off the footbridge? Or do you allow the five to die? The simple facts remain the same: one person must die for five to live. Yet almost nobody is willing to push the man in scenario two. The decision would lead to the same outcome, but in scenario two our emotions are aligned with our rational knowledge that pushing a man from a bridge is and feels wrong.

Fairness is a prerequisite for a successful sustainable democratic system (Villiger, 2015). How fundamentally this is wired into us and moreover, how the feeling of unfairness is a product of our brain structure, is shown in the following example, the 'ultimatum game'. The rules of the game are simple: an experimenter pairs two people together and hands one of them ten dollars. This person (the proposer) gets to decide how the ten dollars are to be divided between the two. The second person (the responder) can either accept the offer, which allows both players to pocket their share, or reject the offer, in which case both players walk away empty-handed. Originally the researchers predicted the proposer would offer only a minimal amount, e.g., one dollar, which the responder would accept, because rejection would leave both players worse off. The researchers soon realized that their predictions were all wrong. Instead of swallowing their pride and pocketing a small profit, the responders typically rejected any offer they perceived as unfair. Proposers anticipated this angry rejection and typically tendered an offer around five dollars. It was such a stunning result and nobody believed it. People almost always made fair offers. The reason the proposer makes a fair offer is that he is able to imagine how the responder will feel about an unfair offer. The responder knows that a low proposal will make the other person angry, which will lead him to reject the offer. As a consequence, the proposer suppresses his greed and equitably splits the ten dollars.

The human ability to sympathize with the feelings of others leads to fairness (Smith, 2000). Then why do we not see more of it in our world of today? We do not have to watch the news to realize that in our everyday lives, moral emotions and sympathizing are limited goods in the global world of people and things. The problem seems to lie with statistics; they do not activate our moral emotions. It is also why doing good must start small. The story of the little boy picking up a starfish from the wet sand and carrying it to the waves striking on the shoreline, moves our souls. While he is delivering a single starfish back to its natural surroundings, a man standing by questions him. "Look around, boy, there are thousands of starfish drying up at low tide on the beach, what you are doing just doesn't make a difference." The boy throws the starfish into the waves, turns and says: "It made a difference to that one."

The need for bonding and true relationships is genetically rooted. Harry F. Harlow, well-known researcher in psychology and behavioural science, showed in his experiments with primates the effect of our social environments on how the plan unfolds: baby monkeys are born with an intense need for attachment. His studies explain that the animals are programmed to seek out love. Baby monkeys cuddled with cloth mothers when in isolation; their craving for affection was stronger than for food. When this need for love was not met, the primates suffered severe side effects and they became like primate psychopaths, completely numb to all expressions of emotions (Wired Humanities Project, 2012). His insights have had an enormous impact on the later understanding of human bonding at young age, specifically in the parent-child relationship.

Albert Jan Dijksterhuis, professor at the Behavioural Science Institute and head of the Social Psychology Department of the Radboud University of Nijmegen, found that the longer people spent analysing their options, the less satisfied they were with their decisions; too many variables and options when shopping overwhelms the rational faculties of our brain and we end up choosing the wrong item. When shopping with too many options, we should just listen to our emotional brain. It is especially useful in helping us make hard decisions. The emotional brain has a massive computational power and quickly assesses alternatives, which are then translated into practical feelings. Our decision then just feels right.

On the other hand, emotions can also lead us astray. Marketeers know this well; they are masters of targeting our feelings and activating those unconscious emotions in us for supporting their messages. All good and clean when controlled and not abused, which seems to be a challenge in the political landscapes of our times: populism is massively taking advantage of our human susceptibility for making decisions in the moment – which we make in a mix of what we feel and what we analytically seem to justify – and abusing our natural tendencies in manipulating the public. Apparently, superpowers are especially susceptible. This cocktail of emotions and rationality benefits us to the maximum, in the one extreme, when using our apparent and tacit knowledge as a shopper in the supermarket, and restrains us to the other extreme, when limiting our mental horizons as through manipulative propaganda. How would our behaviours and human relations at work change when we address these opposing forces in our basic management principles?

HUMAN
RELATIONS
AND
COHERENCE

"A team is a living entity that has a human history, experience, beliefs and needs. As such, it requires attention and caring."

Madeleine Laugeri

In spite of the endless efforts in people-centred management, covered in a multitude of models for continuous improvement, little has changed in the realm of robust human relations at work. Leaders still struggle to find a sound relationship with teams, and team members are unhappy with their boss or their peers and they just shrug their shoulders. All the team building happening has scarcely changed this. There is a whole industry offering programmes for creating high-performing teams: leaders and teams can meet outside of work for some of the most extraordinary and extravagant indoor or outdoor activities. They get to know each other, develop collaboration and sometimes even achieve a certain level of improvement in their relations. The outing ends and people go back to their job. What has changed? How many times have we seen employees and bosses fall back into their old routines in spite of the good intentions and agreed-on action plans during the team-building event? The trouble is that the team members' willingness and capacity to maintain the level of closeness necessary to deliver is not enough. Teams and leaders need cohesion *and* coherence. Coherence is a fundamental and essential ingredient for successful people-centred management. Cohesion, the organization's capacity to quickly and efficiently fulfil the customers' requests, without coherence is a waste of resources. Coherence means people addressing their needs in cooperation and aligning them with the objectives of the organization. If this is not prioritized and ensured, then people will look to spend their time first in satisfying their needs before investing in reaching the objectives. Their emotional state will become the barrier consciously or unconsciously.

Mark Beeman of Northwestern University has shown how people in good moods are significantly better at solving hard problems that require insight. He speculates that this is because the brain areas associated with executive control, such as the prefrontal cortex, are not as preoccupied with managing emotional life. The subject of managing emotional life at work is often treated as a low priority, seen as mingling into a person's private sphere, and triggers at best a pitiful smile at the level of the board of directors. Burnouts must be taken seriously, we are all informed and agree, but still we see unnecessary emotional suffering going on at work. Recent figures show that at least 25% of all employees are stressed and mentally exhausted at their workplace (Gesundheitsförderung Schweiz, 2018).

Hierarchal relationships in this context are a vast, universal subject. Bookshelves are full of literature covering the sociological and behavioural aspects of leadership and YouTube offers a sheer endless quantity of videos and pep talks. It is not easy to find one's way in this jungle. Eric Berne, celebrated psychiatrist and founder of TA (Transactional Analysis), sees group relationships, including the ones at work, constructed in the space and the dynamics around the three boundaries of any organization. He claims that managing these dynamics in order to facilitate robust and sound relationships is elementary for becoming high performing, and organizations must establish a climate of constructive dialogue in the hierarchy, which is one of the key elements in the Emerging Change Model (Laugeri, 2015).

Groups will prosper on emergence, human relations will fundamentally improve, and underperformance will evolve by cohesion (the team's capacity to align its activities in the three contracts to reach the objectives) for results to soar. People will, by themselves, continuously aspire to successful change as a result of the capacity to dialogue in an ok relationship between leaders and teams and coherence will result (alignment of the needs of the team as one entity in cooperation to serve the organization); people will thrive on innovating their work and delivering results, within the organization's customized and agreed-upon frame of control. Emergence is the cement in this mosaic and the oxygen in the beating heart of excellence. Business organizations are well advised to take this into consideration and adapt their leadership styles and teamwork accordingly.

We all have experienced how the leader has a direct impact on the effectiveness of the relationships within a team. Imagine a group of people, a leadership team in a meeting room. It is 9.55am and the meeting should start at 10am. Passionate discussions and debates are ongoing, couples or groups are eager to be heard and all seem to be talking simultaneously; favourite subjects are work, holidays or other events of personal interest. At 10.05am the boss steps in. People take their seats, immediately quiet, and turn their heads to the leader: is he smiling or is there a storm on the horizon? The change of atmosphere is obvious. The leader wishes to start without delay, and the figures of the last, current and coming weeks are on top of the agenda for everybody to see. They are reviewed by overhead projection and are desperately below target. Nobody in the room is happy about the results. The leader asks the team to speak up and comment on the reasons for the difficult situation, but the same group that had a few minutes before been chatting with enthusiasm is now silent.

Some are not really involved, are physically present but mentally elsewhere; they might have been checking their smartphone under the table, hoping nobody notices, or thinking of their weekend activities. Obviously, answering in such a case, without comprehension of the question, is too risky and could result in losing face, favour or even the job. Others are engaged in the subject but do not express themselves and probably wish they were not in the meeting, silently blaming somebody else, maybe the boss, for having made them miss the targets of the week or for some other conflict of a totally different nature. Finally, there are the one or two who save the lot, are fully involved and engaged and enter into discussion. The meeting ends with the issue of an action plan, supervised by the leader and in which the tasks are delegated to the individuals. In the Excel spreadsheet, electronically distributed thereafter, it is not uncommon to see the same name pop up several times under the column 'responsible'. Is this example exaggerated? Astonishingly, I have seen teams and leaders consider this type of interaction and human relations as inevitable and acceptable for getting to excellent results. I disagree. What a waste of time and energy.

According to the survey supporting the 2016 Shift Index issued by Deloitte's Center for the Edge, only 13% of respondents exhibited all three attributes of worker passion: commitment to domain, questing and connecting dispositions (Hagel, Braun, Wooll & de Maar, 2016).

Employees lack motivation and passion, and just a small percentage are able to realize their full potential. It looks like the business world is in a relational crisis. There is an increasing number of employees in organizations who cannot find meaning in their jobs anymore. In local or international companies, the gap between the image of the caring employer that companies try to convey and what employees live in reality, has never been as big, and there is a significant percentage of inactivity spread over all employees (Atmani, 2018). Roland Paulson from Lund University has claimed that, in general, employees pass at least two hours a day at work by doing nothing specifically related to their work. Most of the time inactivity at work is linked to a feeling of frustration in relation to a manager, the whole enterprise or the lack of meaning in the job. It is frightening. At the same time, this presents for any company an enormous opportunity for improvement and potentially gaining a competitive edge.

Many organizations want to motivate by playing the cool card. They offer yoga or table tennis, with the objective of less stress and more engagement at work, both noble and mindful, but how many times have these initiatives produced the desired results? On top, installation of open-space offices, increased delegation of tasks or the implementation of suggestion boxes are praised as the solution for improving the work climate. When companies, however, focus solely on the content of work and the tasks of the job, they will fail in spite of their good intentions. It is not what people need as a priority.

Today, more than ever, people's needs must be taken into consideration for an organization to succeed in its journey to excellence; anything else leads to internal, individual rebellion. It is not the needs of the task but those of human relations that are essential for improving motivation at work. I will advocate that responding to those human relational needs in the first place will resolve the contradiction we have today of the increased wish for people's well-being at work and the decrease of meaning for the individual. Additionally, most organizations tackle the challenge of motivating employees individually and their systems are conceived for this purpose, so I will also advocate that it is high time to put the team at the centre of our organizations to remedy the substantial individual inactivity taking place and to reap the benefits of spending meaningful hours at work.

People, individually or in groups, will structure the time they spend, including at work, to satisfy their needs of stimulation, recognition and structure (Berne, 1963). To be effective and efficient, teams and leaders must be able to align these needs with the strategy and the goals of the organization. This requires sound interaction between all players on a human relations level (Laugeri, 2015). What we see in the example of the weekly meeting, above, is the substantial part of a group satisfying its needs for stimulation through withdrawal or by internal rebellion, rather than by investing efforts in support of the business objectives. We see human relations as a barrier hindering the performance of the group; instead of focusing on what the mission requires, the team and the leader are wasting their and the company's time.

Eric Berne has classified six ways of how individuals will structure time to satisfy their needs: withdrawal, rituals, pastime, activity, games and intimacy. In intimacy, individuals are open for constructive exchange, for acting in the present, in the 'here and now', with authentic feelings and unveiled thinking. It is the powerful catalyst for people to cooperate and spend their time in a result-driven way in their activities. Human relations can reach high performance in these circumstances and a team can act in coherence. The biggest gain an organization can have today is to reduce the amount of people's time wasted and promote intimacy for maximizing the chances of time spent effectively doing work. It ultimately means more output, better results, less stress and less burnout. Figure 1 below shows how a group will achieve more output when its needs in human relations are met and aligned with the objectives of the business. A team reduces or eliminates the time wasted in its perception of the organizational reality and directs its attention subsequently on the activities to fulfil the mission and to reach the organization's goals. Such a group renders its human relations high performing.

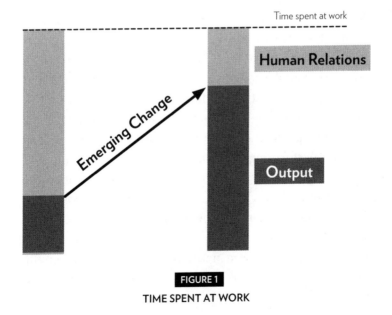

FIGURE 1
TIME SPENT AT WORK

Which steps are we to take? First, we must understand the emotional needs in our relationships (Stewart, 2009). Relational needs show in human interactions. Being aware of these needs in ourselves and in others and the behaviours that follow can help develop and nurture human relationships. Relational needs are emotional needs that can be met through our social connectedness; they are different from those of survival that Abraham Maslow placed at the base of his description of human needs. Often the relational needs are out of our awareness, but we can become conscious of them if they are not being met, a common experience we encounter in our families, our associations, our sports clubs or at work.

The majority of the world's population interacts, at different scales, with strangers, colleagues or friends in the digital world. What is the effect of digitalization on our needs for social connectedness? Digitalization has revolutionized the way we run our world and rendered the opportunities for people to meet face to face at work scarce. The rare time available for employers and employees to invest in building vital, constructive human relations in our professional environment has become extremely valuable. People need to stop wasting their precious time. When investing in high-performing human relations, cooperation will improve and enable the team to use its hours at work more efficiently and reach outstanding results autonomously. The younger generations entering work-life today are asking for this change, and companies better be prepared. Business has witnessed many new models of leadership over the years and still will in the future. Changing sustainably the Swiss way is the approach that enhances those models for the benefit of consistent, exceptional achievements and for respect of our human nature.

We are confronted with a mass and sometimes a mess of information and exchange through the internet. Will future unlimited contact on social media – and we seem to be heading that way – be a valid and full substitution for shaking hands and conversing at a real table? The Chaos Computer Club organized their congress by gathering roughly 15,000 followers in Leipzig. These champions wished to exchange in the real world in person, just like groups of common interest have been doing for centuries. It seems the virtual world cannot satisfy social needs alone (Frey & Osterloh, 2018), and the conclusion is that human beings have a large need for social connectedness that cannot solely be covered by digital media.

These fundamental insights are respected through the Emerging Change Model (Laugeri, 2015). The three contracts of emerging change – vision, mission and cooperation – are the space for a group of people to regularly connect in person and are the means for managing the people's needs and human relationships efficiently, independent of the content of the group's mission. They are an organization's tools to develop cohesion and coherence. They create the space, the responsibilities and the behaviours for dialoguing, and are instrumental for cooperation and for emerging in our organizations, as demonstrated in Swiss democracy.

When relational needs are not met, human beings enter into a mental state of 'not-ok' (Berne, 1963). People become demotivated, frustrated, angry or even aggressive. In spite of the state they are in, people will always try to do the best they can in their own way. They might be inefficient, but they do not come to work to intentionally screw up. In a mental state of 'not-ok', however, coherence in the organization is in danger and attainment of the organization's objectives is at stake. The leader and the team will not work on their mission to the maximum of their potential and this will jeopardize reaching their targets. Organizations with big ambitions and plans for change on their journey to excellence will have no chance in the absence of coherence. There will be little long-lasting success through the changes without coherence. Change programmes then fail, transformations backfire and it is not uncommon to hear, "People initiatives were not managed well."

A report originally published by Booz & Company (Harshak, Aguirre, & Brown, 2010), a global change management survey of 350 senior executives, shows nearly 60% of supervising executives agree that a successful transformation or change programme is due more to people initiatives than any other element. In the same report, it is mentioned that two thirds of transformation programmes fall short of their objectives. Does this mean that in two thirds of the cases supervising executives are not putting the emphasis on people initiatives in their change programme? Certainly not, we would believe, and certainly not what we would expect. Corporate organizations try to give their best in major change initiatives to address all the points taught in and learned from the various 'managing change' books and business schools, including people initiatives. This is, however, many times not enough. The standard reasons people initiatives are missing out on their targets are: team impediments, lack of freedom for decision-making, not learning from each other, functional silos, missed collaboration between team and management or no cooperation on the team. These are symptoms of a disrupted human process with a deficit in addressing the relational needs of a group. The main grounds, however, of why people initiatives do not satisfy, is because of what they are: initiatives. The needs of a group must be dealt with sustainably, in a continuous manner, in the daily interactions, in its activities and disregarding this fact will ultimately lead to a loss of coherence in the organization. When a group lacks coherence, things turn sour. All the good intentions and energy put into the changes and the people initiatives, from the CEO to the shop floor, are in vain, if on completion of the change programme coherence is not sustainably addressed. The absence of coherence leads inevitably to the next restructuring program with disastrous losses for the company and the employees.

How this destroys value, big time, is illustrated in the fate of a once-successful ice cream company. In this case, a stand-alone ice cream street sales business, supplied by its two dedicated factories, is integrated into a new regional structure. The new structure is headed by a regional CEO and his direct reports – the country, business and operations managers – are aligned behind the objectives for the region. The profit margins of the street sales are strikingly above average in the industry.

After a while of business as usual, sales, unexpectedly, start eroding and the bottom line gets slowly under pressure. The strategic unit of operations at the head office is asked for help and starts an analysis. It proclaims, among other measures, the reduction of fixed costs, with the classic idea of merging the two ice cream factories.

The comparison of production costs leads to the proposal of closing the factory in the south and investing in the factory in the north. Business management located in the south intervenes, and after a second analysis the decision is reversed: the factory in the north shall be shut down.

A project is kicked off, including people initiatives. The process of quitting production in the one factory and investing in the other is initiated. Installations, modifications and start-up of the new lines are to be realized fast, because the products must be ready for the coming ice cream season in six months. Pressure is high and the CEO of the region is pushing. The business manager, technical manager, factory manager, supply chain manger, head of engineering and their staff are working and following the substantial changes in the factory together. They are all fully engaged and intervene in the best interests and capabilities, staying optimistic in spite of the many problems and concerns in their individual areas of activities, for no one wants to disappoint the CEO. Issues, escalated by the supervisors, the shop floor and the project teams, are addressed during the monthly business management meetings and treated with an action, reported in an action plan for completion by an imposed date. This game goes on for a while until all the accumulated failures and inconsistencies in the project cannot be played down anymore, neither by the project nor the business management and one day it becomes evident that production will not be ready for the next ice cream season.

All levers are pulled to improve the new installations and to find alternative sourcing. Unfortunately, the business runs out of time. The ice cream season arrives, the factory does its best to supply, but substandard performance in production and quality problems of the products in the market compromise deliveries and in the aftermath of this turmoil important sales are lost, not to be recovered. The former highly profitable ice cream business quickly generates substantial financial losses, and nobody understands why. An immediate internal audit is launched. The factory manager is fired and the factory reorganized, shedding lines and products to focus on the most profitable stock keeping units (SKUs). The motivation of the factory's supervisors and workforce suffers, key people quit and production performance decreases even more. Significant amounts of cash and time are invested over the following 12 months to save the business, albeit without success. First the business manager, then the regional CEO leave the company. A few years later, the local business, having faced huge losses, in millions of euros, not to mention the enormous waste of the employees' efforts and competencies, is restructured. The factory is shut down, production integrated into neighbouring countries and the business merged into other markets.

The internal audit revealed all the common errors and mistakes that we have seen so many times made in project management. The essence, however, of what went wrong, when reading between the lines, was to be found in the human relationships of leaders and teams and it started at the top. The CEO and the top management were lacking federating forces and autonomy in their human relations; cooperation on the team and constructive dialoguing of the group as one entity with the leader were totally missing. The business manager of street sales, after the regional integration, realized he had lost flexibility in responding to demand, the crucial element for competing in the market he was operating. He was not aligned with the new technical requirements introduced by the region and was not really supportive of merging his supplying factories. Instead of addressing his concerns in the group, he was in a psychological game of second degree. The factory manager in the south, as it turned out, had promised unrealistic production costs during the second analysis for comparison, which had led to the closure of the factory in the north. He was seeking to render the operation competitive, pleasing his boss and looking for recognition in the implementation of an oversized and unwarranted distribution centre and a mass of crowded shop-floor installations. The technical manager was promoted and transferred to the global business unit once the shut-down of the factory in the north had been announced and the newcomer was not ok with the project management. The chief engineer was close to retirement and far from the project site, located at another head office outside of the region. He meant to realize a speedy and most harmonious project completion, mentally denying the seriousness and severity of the situation and did not speak up early enough. What had happened? Everyone believed he was doing the best he could in his situation, but because the relational needs as a management team were not addressed, each individual was acting in an individual way, misaligned and increasingly diverging from what the organization wanted to achieve. Human relations in the group and with the leader, the CEO, were not addressed sustainably and became strongly underperforming which obviously cascaded into the whole organization. The managers wasted time, satisfying their own needs and causing management paralysis with disastrous consequences for the company. The tragedy of annihilating a whole business, damaging careers, destroying jobs and putting the livelihood of hundreds in danger became reality.

The course of events in the ice cream case is shown in Figure 2. When an organization is built, e.g., in a new structure or with a change program in an existing structure, the company will launch the necessary people initiatives and the leaders and teams will follow an initial alignment of their needs with the objectives (Step 1). People will subsequently develop and perform, in their best of interests, by deploying their talents and following their preferences within their understanding of what is required and what their needs are. Our world is full of good intentions on the one hand, and of disorder and barriers between human beings on the other; this will naturally lead to divergence in the organization.

In the ice cream case, the CEO, as well as the business, factory and technical managers, were all convinced of their decisions and actions to render the organization more flexible and more profitable.

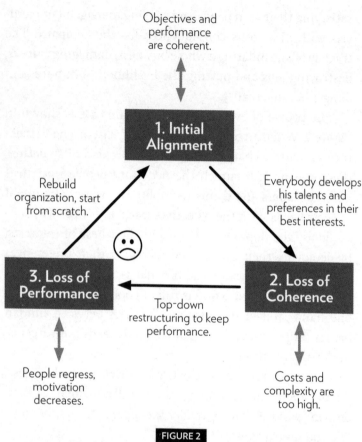

FIGURE 2

TRADITIONAL CHANGE PROCESS WITHOUT COHERENCE

In reality, the team was not in the 'here and now'. Everyone in isolation was adding his part in creating a disrupted human process, where the relational needs were satisfied individually, while the organization was requiring speedy performance of the combined workforce. Loss of coherence (Step 2) happens when divergence induces a misalignment of the team's relational needs and the manner in which they are satisfied from what the objectives of the organization impose or require. As a result, time and effort are wasted, complexity in the organization increases, costs rise, results are out of line and top-down intervention becomes a necessity with the aim to reinstall the desired performance. Management calls for a quick remedy with the launch of improvement projects and the company expects fast results; they, however, are not sustainable without coherence, so motivation suffers and the workforce regresses further. The organization experiences bigger losses of performance (Step 3), calling for more drastic changes. Restructuring is introduced with huge efforts and costs, certainly on the human side, and people initiatives are again big on the agenda. A new organization is built, an effort is undertaken to align and the process continues. If in the initial alignment coherence is still not ensured, the organization enters into a vicious circle. Nobody wants this to happen, and still it does. The question is: how can a vicious circle be avoided or, moreover, how can organizations achieve a virtuous circle where performance consistently increases, and top-down restructuring is avoided?

There is a long list of management books that offer successful change management methods and models. Some are famous. Most of them concentrate on how to move from Step 3 to Step 1 in the diagram above. Organizations move from loss of performance (even if it is not yet visible to all) to a level where leaders and teams are aligned behind the objectives and where performance is within expectations. That is very good. Then the book or video finishes with 'embedding change in the organization', 'make it stick' or 'culture change', offering, however, much less on how this is done. What a pity. When, after the change is installed, the organization follows the same path that led to the loss of performance in the first place – focusing exclusively on managing by objectives and disregarding the priority of managing the needs of the people – then the next restructuring project is already assured.

Installing high-performing human relations is the fundamental condition for managing coherence and for changing sustainably. It is simple, and once its active management is initiated and first fruits harvested, the benefits become normal and evident for all who are involved; people then are prone to believe it had always been that way. So why is coherence not high on the agenda of our enterprises? There is doubt from the managers: human relations are not part of traditional management. Bosses associate working on high-performing human relations with touchy-feely stuff, and many believe that their natural soft skills as leaders will suffice. It took me a while to understand how wrong that is. It is not about being liked by all or making everybody happy. Installing and sustaining high-performing human relations requires an array of tangible and concrete skills and procedures. High-performing human relations does not mean avoiding conflicts; instead, the relations enable correct and efficient treatment – that is why they are high performing. I have seen the regular tendency of losing coherence in organizations because, contrarily to common belief, the needs in human relations do not just manage themselves. We cannot allow the loss of coherence to happen in the first place and we must anticipate the future.

There is a simple method applicable in any organization to address the demands of managing coherence, independently of the nature of the objectives of the organization: a human process with emerging change (Laugeri, 2015). This approach allows teams and leaders to create and sustain coherence in a natural way, making changing sustainable, and starts with two concepts: autonomy and cooperation. I believe this manner of leading represents yet another paradigm shift in our journey to excellence, and we should listen to those coming into business nowadays who are telling us that this shift is timely.

5

AUTONOMY AND COOPERATION

"Because the organizational boundaries delimit the space for team membership, a cooperation contract exists in any group, just by the fact that the group exists. Nobody can force a team to formalize it and nobody can stop the team from formalizing it either."

Madeleine Laugeri

We have seen that the evolution of the Swiss direct democracy and its process of changing sustainably, the Swiss way, was powered by emergence based on autonomy, cooperation and constructive dialogue, those drivers for cohesion and coherence that are central to the approach of emerging change (Laugeri, 2105). The advantages of these democratic principles for a business on its journey to excellence, comprising individual freedom with common objectives, is expressed by other authors. Charles Handy refers to reverse delegation in a democracy (Handy, 1994) and makes the connection to the organizational environment in business. Power is situated naturally at the lowest possible level of an organization, where the appropriate expertise and competencies are located, where the activity is performed. This direct responsibility goes well with the different models of autonomy on the factory shop floor. Handy applies democratic principles, as described here in the examples of the Swiss democracy, to businesses or organizations in general. Federalism is the system of dual citizenship, where an individual takes responsibility for his or her actions while being part of a bigger common purpose; as Helmut Maucher, late CEO of Nestlé, said: "Think global, act local."

Analogies between the call for direct democracy and for a paradigm shift of leadership toward people-centred management in business are not by chance. They are built on the same premises of individual freedom and responsibilities. According to Kaspar Villiger, former federal councillor of Switzerland, democracies have sustainably higher growth rates and prosperity than authoritarian systems. He carves out in *Democracy and Conceptual Thinking* the four driving forces that interact in a modern direct democracy:

- People
- Institutions
- Culture
- Coincidence

Humans have a natural preference for fairness, a tendency which has its origins in the phylogeny of our species; it is a product of our biological evolution and this must be taken into consideration in our economic and political environment. There is no stability if the order in society is perceived as unfair. Only when fairness is ensured can a democracy be built successfully on the autonomy of the people, people who are self-responsible, whose dignity is inviolable and whose moral framework guides toward acceptable conduct. Villiger claims autonomy within this frame as the base for a prosperous democratic society. He sees a strong interaction between economic and political institutions, which together must decide whether the state creates prosperity or slides into poverty. These exchanges need to be managed dynamically, in response to the constant need for adapting to the developments a state is faced with. Common identity and culture require clear boundaries in a political structure as well as within the teams of an organization, and here Villiger crosses paths with Eric Berne, founder of Transactional Analysis. Berne distinguishes between three boundaries in any organization (Berne, 1963): the external, the major internal and the minor internal. A group of people such as a team with a leader will need to manage their relations by the dynamics going on at these boundaries. The external boundary is the membrane between the group and the environment.

The dynamics of hierarchical relationships happen at the major internal boundary and the interactions among peers take place at the minor internal boundary.

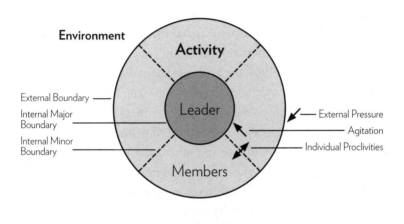

FIGURE 3
STRUCTURE AND DYNAMICS OF AN ORGANIZATION (BERNE, 1963)

Our cultural incentives and our common values, which have evolved during the history of humanity, have a strong influence on how people will behave and how they will relate at these boundaries. Villiger goes on, "Values such as trust and confidence are just as important for sustainable economic success as for political advancements, and our political leaders must respect this." In a democracy, like in business, we need to be ready for the unforeseen and there coincidence will continue to play an important role – coincidence as in the emergence of new opportunities and new constellations. The political system must be such that the people are well prepared to grasp the opportunity or dismiss the idea based on a high degree of freedom and prior acquisition of knowledge on the issue, notwithstanding that having the right leader at the right time will not lose importance. When listening to Villiger, the arguments for a sustainably successful democracy are unmistakably just as valid for any people-centred organization, including, of course, any business organization.

By the early 1990s, we had established a group of internal consultants at the global head office. They were supporting a company-wide initiative to install a continuous improvement process. The group had grown to more than 30 persons, all very young and evaluated as high potentials at the beginning of their careers. They were hand-picked and subject to several days of interactive recruitment, some of them coming directly from university and others with work experience. Their mission was to move around the world, split up into six teams, and conduct improvement projects within our production organization comprising 500 factories. Each project normally lasted several months, during which the factories and adjacent operational units were supposed to generate immediate productivity improvements. It was a unique set-up for two reasons. First, the company was very much decentralized, and teams sent from the centre were considered experts, which gave even to these youngsters a special authority within the organization. There was a savings report going to the global head of operations and once a year directly to the CEO. Second, the teams were intended to help and not audit the factories.

Group members were representing a new generation of professionals using new tools and methods, questioning the status quo and searching for innovative solutions on the journey to excellence. The projects received the first six laptops with built-in modems ever purchased by the organization and so we had 24-hour contact by email with each of the six teams anywhere in the world where there was a working phone line. It's hard to believe, but at the time this was a huge innovation in communication; our solution would be called primitive today. Dialling-in over the phone took forever and lines would collapse exactly when important messages were about to be exchanged. We were using a home-grown email software, running on mainframes and a word processing program, forcing the user to restart every time he made a mistake. There was no network of servers. The word software was jargon, the importance of Microsoft was only known to IT professionals in the company and 'Outlook' was an activity for forecasting the yearly figures. And even so, we were then at the forefront of the digital revolution at our head office.

The methods applied to the projects had been developed from novel management tools for operational improvements, e.g., waste analysis, information flow analysis ('brown paper'), time studies, capacity analysis, small group and team-building activities, internal and external customer satisfaction surveys or business process analysis. The whole library was considered as expertise and highly confidential, so distribution out of the unit was restricted. With the deployment of the group over the years, other methods – TPM (Total Productive Maintenance) or Lean Management – were introduced and adapted to perfection along the company's needs and wishes. In the beginning, the factories received the teams from the centre correctly, with scepticism and once in a while as intruders. "What did these youngsters from head office know about the operations of the locals? What kind of credibility did they have and what kind of help could one expect? Were they not auditors?" We quickly realized that any success would only happen if the locals and the teams from the centre worked together.

We started to communicate cooperation and collaboration through the local units and hierarchy right down to the shop floor. The projects were initiated with a kick-off meeting where the visiting productivity team showed PowerPoint slides of the expected course of the project in the presence of the factory management and the supervisors; the latter, especially curious of what was to come, with arms crossed, lips tight and dressed in their work clothes of different colours, representing the different departments, e.g., blue for maintenance, brown for production. The teams had more or less six months to apply the methods, collaborate with the factory's workforce, implement changes and create improvements; we normally did achieve some sort of collaboration and operational improvements and we showed savings. Each project was revisited a year later for a follow-up of the accomplishments made during the project or the changes, as agreed to by the locals, to be installed thereafter. So, how well did we do? Top management was excited and very happy about the whole approach and the results we published; the international business school close by our head office demonstrated strong interest in our team and invited us to share our modus operandi and experiences with their participants. It was not very common in those days for big corporations to have improvement projects launched in-house by a group of internal consultants; most companies hired well-known consulting firms for the purpose.

What did the factories say to the project results? The response was mixed. In our yearly reviews, we found that some projects had created lasting improvements whereas others were back to square one after the project team had left and, in some cases, one area was successful and another not, within the same factory. We asked the clients and ourselves what was missing when the change was not sustained. Our methods were identical for all teams and even their application was tightly controlled by the project leaders and by the centre and there were regular visits from the head office to this end. We were giving technical training and workshops for improved skills, relationships and interactions during the projects. Our initiatives of management commitment and employee involvement were communicated in the local organizations from the top to the shop floor. The managers were asked to empower their employees and people were consistently proclaimed as the company's biggest asset. Our company values and beliefs were people- and family-oriented and strongly present, and we tried to foster cooperation in the teams and in the projects. The teams were working autonomously and independently and decisions and responsibilities on how to achieve savings and engage factory people were delegated to the lowest levels. Project leaders, on the other hand, were defining the work plans, setting the objectives and controlling the activities of the team members closely. Motivation on the team was high, so working long hours during the project covering different shifts in the factories was generally not an issue. Everyone seemed heavily committed to deliver and achievement in relation to the plan was reviewed daily by the team.

There were still, however, substantial differences in the results between projects. It seemed that in some instances, teams and factory people cooperated successfully, in others less so. Obviously, the behaviour of the project leader and the team members had a strong influence on how the factory would develop, accept and then realize the improvement proposals. Clearly, there was divergence between and within projects on how the people were involved, behaved and treated each other. But still, we wondered why some teams sustained cooperation and others did not and what the reasons were for people to continue improving autonomously in one area but not in another. For us, autonomy meant giving a frame to all employees in the factory to participate freely. We proclaimed trust and honesty when working together within this frame, which we realized was more than just following an action plan for autonomous completion of a task. We were aware that we had to concentrate on how we behaved and respected our clients and ourselves. But did we actively consider and were we thoughtful enough of the needs of the people in the factory and basics of human interactions during our interventions to be able to reach the project's targets together and for the factory to continue the desired improvement process?

Robert Fulghum sums up the fundamentals of human interactions nicely in his book *All I Really Need to Know I Learned in Kindergarten*. His stories give us a view of the basic moral of transparent human interaction, of mutual understanding and appreciation. His wisdom is eternal and goes to the heart in his writing, 'These are the things I learned':

"Share everything – Play fair – Don't hit people – Put things back where you found them – Clean up your own mess –

Don't take things that aren't yours – Say you're sorry when you hurt somebody – Wash your hands before you eat – Flush – Warm cookies and cold milk are good for you – Live a balanced life, learn some and think some and draw and paint and sing and dance and play and work every day some – Take a nap every afternoon – When you go out in the world, watch out for traffic, hold hands and stick together – Be aware of wonder." (Fulghum, 1990).

Yes, it sounds cosy and comforting, just like milk and cookies, for sure. But is it just kindergarten talk and totally irrelevant to the serious world of adults? I believe not. Taking this on board at face value to inform how we interact in the space of competition and the field of rough and risky business will seem ridiculous to any business manager or improvement project member. That is not the point. Fulghum's anecdotes of the real world around his 'These are the things I have learned' are metaphors that are more than just food for thought. The universal morals Fulghum shares act as a reminder of basic, sound human interactions even if only unconsciously, and our professional lives in our organizations should not be an exception. A future where organizations do not only talk about the human side of management but actually live it will require that the interactions of teams and leaders do not contradict with the basics of what deep down we as human beings morally and emotionally need to respect, regardless of the business objectives or the operational mission. These basics are essentially contained in the term autonomy, as defined by Transactional Analysis (Berne, 1963). Autonomy covers the three elements of *clear consciousness, spontaneity* and *intimacy*. Clear consciousness is the faculty of experiencing our surroundings in our own way and not through what others are expecting from us.

It is what we call being in the 'here and now'. Spontaneity is the ability to choose what we feel and not be bogged down in psychological games. Intimacy is the freedom to show nearness between humans, expressed in affection and positive feelings for creating trust.

Our moral mind is genetically rooted, and we all carry the building plan and the needs for moral behaviour in us. Through our education and upbringing, we have learned to respect these moral frameworks and rules in our day-to-day life from the very fundamentals such as the Bible's Ten Commandments to the more specialized ones, e.g., Adolph Freiherr Knigge's rules of good manners. They allow for us to survive together in all kinds of environments in the most harmonious way with the least of social defects. Why then do we tend to forget these basics when we act as leaders in business? They often go under in the vast amount of knowledge and experience that we carry around in our individual mental backpacks. Our 'house of knowledge and experience' is created by a multitude of teachers consciously and unconsciously: family, kin, friends in schools and universities, and all of our managers and colleagues we encountered in our jobs. Sometimes this house has walls so thick that they bar us from encountering anything other than our own one-sided perspective on moral and human interaction created in our own messy world of emotions and rationality. We carry these walls around within us, including at work in our organizations. What would happen if we made a hole in the bricks? What have these barriers hindered us from seeing? How should we remove them? Why not apply the "wisdom of knowing how to live, what to do and how to be," as Robert Fulghum puts it? It is clear that we cannot run an organization based on this wisdom alone; however, it can create the urge in our daily professional and private lives to establish robust relationships.

In *From Leadership-as-Practice to Leaderful Practice*, Joseph A. Raelin calls for a leadership style favouring a humble posture that can only be described as 'being in the world'. He states that we should not privilege influence as the predominant mode of engagement in leadership, which fits well with the concept of autonomy and makes sense not only in the interaction between leader and employee but should also be strongly applicable to the relationships in teams. Influence among peers is only constructive, then, when there is no doubt in the relationships. This is crucial in the context of yet other evidence, shared by Jon R. Katzenbach and Douglas K. Smith in *The Wisdom of Teams: Creating the High-Performance Organization* (2005), where they write: "Real teams are the most successful spearheads of change at all levels; working in teams naturally integrates performance and learning. Teams have a unique potential to deliver results and many benefits, e.g., development of members and stronger company-wide performance."

We have all heard, "The whole is more than the sum of its parts," and Michael Tomasello shows how fundamental this wisdom is to our human nature (Tomasello, 2008). The behaviours necessary for cooperation seem to be founded in the origin of our species. Michael Tomasello explains the phylogenetic origin of cooperation and collaboration in his fascinating studies with young human children and primates. "Young human children are naturally cooperative and helpful in many, though not all, situations. And they do not get this from adults; it comes naturally." Tomasello adds,

"Children's relatively indiscriminate cooperativeness will begin to be mediated by such things as their judgment of likely reciprocity and their concern for how others in the group judge them, which were instrumental in the evolution of humans' natural cooperativeness in the first place. And they will begin to internalize many culturally specific social norms for how we do things, how one ought to do things, if one is to be a member of this group." In other words: cooperation comes naturally before culture. He mentions how children's natural behaviour to help is intrinsically rewarding, and rewarding helping does not activate children's motivation for helping, but may even undermine it. "Interestingly," he writes, "the early helping of children is not a behaviour created by a socialization process, rather an outward expression of a natural tendency to sympathize with others having problems." His studies show the significance of moral frames and social norms for a group to get the necessary mileage out of this natural tendency.

Cooperation and collaboration with leaders and in teams in complex organizations often turn out otherwise. And it would be too easy to believe that the phylogenetic origin of cooperation, although the idea is quite fascinating, would still be dominating our behaviours as adults. There are plenty of reasons extracted from sociology, psychology and other disciplines that can explain why. It is not my intention to investigate these barriers further, as the purpose of this book is to focus on how teams and leaders can mobilize our natural tendencies for helping and cooperation by applying the Emerging Change Model (Laugeri, 2015). One specific hindrance to cooperation that is in place in many of our organizations of today and which comes to my mind in this context are the individual evaluation schemes. (It could look like we are making too big a jump from the depth of human science to empiric observations by the practitioner; I believe, however, we can give ourselves the permission to single out actual cases by experience.) The attractive benefits of individual appreciation schemes in terms of remuneration and recognition have become counterproductive to the original need and unique potential of cooperation between human beings. And it looks like the closer to the top, the more influence they have.

Michael Tomasello shows how group processes evolved naturally out of the activities of early humans, where interdependency was a key driver for group members to achieve a common goal: food. Supported by his studies, he points out an important physiological characteristic that is potentially connected to our natural cooperativeness and can be imagined as a clear evolutionary benefit: All two hundred species of nonhuman primates have basically dark eyes with the white sclera barely visible. The white sclera of humans is about three times larger, making the human gaze much more easily detectable by *others*. As Tomasello writes, for following gaze direction, chimpanzees rely almost exclusively on head direction, whereas human infants rely mainly on eye direction. "One can imagine in evolution why it is of benefit for you to be able to follow my eye direction easily – to spy predators or food, for example – but nature cannot select the whiteness of my eyes based on some advantage to you; it must be of some advantage to me ... my eye direction for all to see could have evolved only in a cooperative social environment in which others were not likely to exploit it to my detriment ...

(but) to our mutual benefit." First, though, there had to be an initial condition that allowed the move from competing to cooperation, from the 'I' to the 'we' mode. Here Tomasello identifies tolerance and trust as key actors, and although it seems unclear how they evolved in the phylogenesis of humans, there is the belief that it must have involved those parts of the human brain related to emotions.

All modern people-centred management principles cannot disregard these two values and should feel comforted and encouraged, knowing that they are of natural origin in humans for cooperating in a team. Tomasello refers to two other evolutionary prerequisites in human beings for cooperation and collaboration: skills and motivations for 'shared intentionality' and group-level institutional practices involving social norms and institutional roles. The latter being a condition *sine qua non* of our cultural evolution and the reason for its increased speed versus biological evolution. "Because of this fact," Tomasello writes, "presumably a characteristic of no other species, a new process of cultural group selection became possible."

Already in 1977, Konrad Lorenz postulated in *Die Rückseite des Spiegels*: "Humans have become cultural beings through their phylogenetic evolution. The new structures the human brain has developed under evolutionary selection and through accumulating traditional knowledge is not a cultural, moreover a phylogenetic, process triggered by the emergence of cognitive skills." Cooperation is a product of our phylogeny and our interactive accumulation of traditional knowledge; it might be a surprise in the societies of today, but the origin of human cooperation is of a biological nature. A team's autonomy to cooperate is based on a long series of emerging attributes in the evolution of our species involving our emotions, values and interactions as human beings. There is one remarkable conclusion to this fact: when people have the option, there is absolutely no leader required for them to cooperate.

Konrad Lorenz uses the term 'fulguration'. Fulgurations, or innovations, bring about the unforeseeable changes in our world such as the developments the brain has gone through from the pre-human to its current evolutionary state. Innovations emerge and produce successes and failures, sometimes hard to accept. Emergence makes changing sustainable: one single new advancement is autonomously deduced out of all the previous evolutionary steps following the same set of fundamental laws and principles. As Philip Warren Anderson, celebrated theoretical physicist and 1977 Nobel prize winner, writes in "More Is Different" (1972): "The whole becomes not only more than but very different from the sum of its parts." We have evolved from less to more complex systems and at each new level of complexity entirely new properties appear. Anderson states: "Understanding of the new behaviours requires research that I think is as fundamental in its nature as any other ... The workings of our minds and bodies, and of all the animate and inanimate matter of which we have any detailed knowledge, are assumed to be controlled by the same set of fundamental laws, which except under certain extreme conditions we feel we know pretty well" (Anderson, 1972). It follows that we can reduce a current state to a previous one; however, we cannot reconstruct the nature of the present or the future from the knowledge of those laws. It is a one-way street. Before change emerges, we do not know what to expect; it is a universal and irrefutable fact.

In his book *Leading Self-Organising Teams*, Siegfried Kaltenecker writes, "The best architectures, require-ments and designs emerge from self-organizing teams" (Kaltenecker, 2015). He adds: "Knowledge workers have to manage themselves. They have to have autonomy." The importance of high-performing teams is common wisdom in sports, and the understanding of teamwork can vary considerably between sport disciplines. In his example of soccer, Kaltenecker shows us that leadership is a team sport. During a soccer game, the teams playing on the field are on their own. The coach is at the sideline and is observ-ing the activities of the game. Now that is not always true; we have all seen coaches jump up from the players' bench and yell onto the soccer field. However, such actions are, in the eyes of the expert, questionable and seldom beneficial to the overall objectives. When the game is on, the team is usually organizing its own playing and deciding on its actions to win by itself. As a matter of fact, any outside intervention, not only from the coach, can be detrimental to the team's performance: respecting the team's auton-omy when it is in its activities is crucial for its success. The coach can exchange players or give feedback in the locker room before and after the game or during half-time. But during the time the players are on the field, they are on their own.

Sports do deliver a bunch of great analogies that help us understand different principles of autonomy and coop-eration and the unique potential teams have for achieving outstanding results. Top-league sports clubs have long surpassed the idea of playing just for enjoyment and are big business today. They compare to any other corporate organization in terms of management, employees, consumers, customers and suppliers, communication and administration. Their road to excellence is also about people-centred management. When watching American football, we can identify how high-performing teams tick. In American football we see the interaction of those different complementary dynamics that are also present and essential in any business organization on its journey to excellence.

First, there is process orientation. American football is a close-to-perfect representation of how a team is organized around agreed-on processes. They are called plays. An American football team has to master its plays. They are designed, trained and applied in a truly unmistakable and no-deviation manner, and there are process owners, e.g., the offence coordinator for 'play offence' and the defence coordinator for 'play defence'. These leaders carry the ultimate responsibility for design and development, viability and effectiveness of their processes, which they ensure during training camp and preseason, relying on a bag full of key people internally and externally. They are also responsible to the head coach for managing the coherence of the team's needs in their activities and the vision and strategy of the organization and consequently the operational delivery during the season.

The second dynamic of a successful football team is training. Process owners ensure the right training of the players to build the knowledge and skills needed in their process. An American football team has three distinct teams of players. During the game, an offence team faces an adversary defence team on the field. The aim of the offence team is to score points by transporting the football from the one end of the field to the adversary end.

The defence team obviously must prevent this from happening. At certain stages in the game, these teams can be supported by a third group known as the special team. It consists of players who are responsible for performing kick-offs, punts and field goals. Teams are exchanged on the field during the game depending on who has the right to play offence, who is in defence and which tasks need completion. These activities are covered by a precise set of rules that are reinforced by several referees during a game. The players represent a multitude of different roles and each role has its pattern of skills and competencies needed in the activities. Players are therefore trained on specific tasks essential for the corresponding process to deliver the expected results.

Professional American football is a rough and tough sport. Footballers are exceptional athletes and undergo extensive preparation and training. The rules of the game allow for violent encounters between players of adversary teams in such a way that risks of significant bodily harm cannot be excluded, even to the correctly prepared. Training of physical, technical, tactical and mental strength in a specific role is of utmost importance for the player and the team and is given the necessary management focus by the process owners. The combination of this high level of competencies, skills and knowledge for all players in each role with the unique and competitive design of the processes are primordial for sustainable success of the team. Obviously the better this works in synergy, the better chances are for the team to become excellent. The head coach, who is the overall responsible leader during the game, is the process owner for 'winning the game'.

He makes sure that all processes, the required responses to the strategic elements of the environment, the knowledge and skills of the players come together for a given game. How does this work?

The Philadelphia Eagles' offence and the New England Patriots' defence teams position themselves on the field and are facing each other at the line of scrimmage and the players, with the energy of giant coiled springs, are ready to leap into the game. Nobody moves until the starting signal is given. Muscles are tense and bulging in the tight and short-sleeved uniform, and the fierce look of adversaries facing mask to mask are displayed in the camera's closeup. Only the tight ends are moving left or right behind the line to confuse the adversary. Every player, in his position, is prepared to pounce into the play as required by his role, his responsibilities and the agreed-on process. We are watching the 52nd Super Bowl in history, the prestigious, annual championship final of the NFL, the National Football League.

There are 2 minutes and 25 seconds left in the game. The score is 32 to 33 for the Patriots. They are the favourites to win, but the game's outcome is still open, meaning it could go either way. Tension is rising throughout the stadium. The Eagles' offensive holds the ball on the 12-yard line with a third down; they are in charge of the next step on the field and the coaches can only observe. The team's concentration is fully on the initiation of the play, and suddenly the quarterback makes the call. In a flash, the centre at the line of scrimmage fires the ball backwards between his legs, directly into the quarterback's open hands. This is the signal both teams have been waiting for: in a split second tons of human mass run, tackle, block or smash into each other and floods of adrenalin pour through the veins of players, coaches, fans and managers. The Eagles' quarterback, Nick Foles, catches the football from the centre, fires it to tight end, Zack Ertz, who snatches it out of its trajectory and runs. After rushing several yards, he takes a giant leap over the attacking defence player, stretches in horizontal flight toward the end zone, dives and hits the ground for a touchdown. The touchdown is confirmed, and points awarded to the Eagles. They now have the chance for the 'extra point', but Foles throws an incomplete pass and the Patriots regain ball possession.

The Eagles are now, after only four seconds of play, leading the game with a 5-point difference and there are 2 minutes and 21 seconds still to go. The Patriots' offence team has been called onto the field; they need to complete their drive to a touchdown to over-score their opponent in the remaining 2 minutes and few seconds of the game. Normally this is a feasible task and Tom Brady, star quarterback of the Patriots, starts things off with an eight-yard completion. It looks like everything is lined up for the Patriots. On his second down, he receives the ball from the centre and is searching the field in the few seconds available to cast his decisive pass to a potential receiver. Suddenly, in a shocking reversal, the crucial game-changing event happens. Brady is sacked by the Eagles' defence team. The ball is knocked away, out of Brady's grasp, by Brandon Graham, fumbled and caught by Derek Barnett of the Eagles' defence in a perfect example of the defence's autonomous cooperation, and the Eagles have regained ball possession. "Brandon Graham made the play to win it," Barnett told reporters after the game. "It was a good bounce. Right into my hands"

(Kaplan, 2018). Was this pure coincidence for Barnett to be there in the right place at exactly the right time? I think not. In a high-performing team with autonomous cooperation, doing the right thing just feels right. In the aftermath of the critical interception, time runs out for the Patriots to turn the ship around and the Philadelphia Eagles, the underdog, win Super Bowl LII.

Not only sports fans are impressed by the professionalism and the precision both teams reveal when demonstrating their outstanding plays and skills. It is a respect often shared, independently of who won or lost, and it brings us to how a team's heart beats for excellence. Such a high-performing team exerts a powerful and essential force not always explicitly visible to the spectator's eye, although once mentioned, everybody kind of agrees to its evidence: the *interdependency* among the players during the play. Unfortunately, it does not sound too spectacular, and we all take it for granted. Interdependency is the vivid expression of a team trusting each other. It is probably the most impactful team quality and coaches know how much attention it needs. Each player must rely on each of his team's colleagues and each sequence, in every play, requires 100% concentration. Once the ball is launched, there is no time to think rationally or to focus on anything else than one's own responsibilities. There are only a few seconds at their disposal to be successful as a team and each and every one of the players must trust his colleague for his performance. Decisions are made instantaneously. The emotional part of the brain is highly activated, and failure comes at a high price; in such a case, not only would the team be losing opportunities for scoring and reward, a player might experience serious injuries, too. The quarterback, wide receiver, tight end and running back are fully concentrated on their activity to throw, run or catch the ball; they cannot focus on all the dangers they might be facing. In other words, their teammates have to take care of them. All players have the responsibility to perform flawlessly in their activity, on which the team must rely without hesitation, for a quarterback might not realize that an opponent, a defence player of 120kg of muscles and bones, is approaching at near to freight-train speed. If so, he will not be prepared for the impact should he be hit, which can have disastrous consequences. He must rely on those on the team who intervene and block the approach of the adversary and make sure he can perform his part of the process to perfection, at best of his skills and competencies without being seriously injured. Continuous repetition during preparation and the adjacent rituals and routines develop and confirm a common understanding and consciousness of how every player is permitted to focus on his job.

American football is a great example of what trust does to cooperation; high performance in the 'here and now' fits perfectly into a play of a few seconds. Such a task requires a shared goal, clear boundaries and unconditional investment of each individual to the team. In prehistoric times, commitment to cooperation and total reliance prevailed among a group of hunters, making the kill of a mammoth possible (Tomasello, 2008). There was too much at risk for the individual in case of team failure, a human gamble we still encounter today in our daily lives, although in a totally different context. In American football, the delivery of a play is reduced to a time span of a few seconds, where trust is the primary condition in the heartbeat of excellence. Personal investment into concentrating on one's own responsibilities and the robustness of the mutual interactions among peers, elevate the team to unknown heights of performance. The team's decisions are highly influenced by emotions and the feeling of doing the right thing together prevails. Autonomy and clear consciousness, interdependency and robust human relationships, intimacy and spontaneity deliver a human process permitting the team to succeed, a human process which is supported by rituals and routines. Coaches know this and have the players learn to trust and rely on each other over and over again, a fundamental part of the team's preparation for the players to create their autonomy. The coaches do not intervene during the play, they just couldn't in the few seconds available. Once in the game, the team must organize its activities within the established relational frame. Such a team is self-organizing, admittedly with fewer degrees of freedom than in a business organization, and it is also high performing. High-performing teams work along agreed-on processes, have the required knowledge and skills and cooperate in autonomy of their human relations while benefitting from the power of their emotional brain. What can we draw from the sports example of autonomy, cooperation and collaboration? How can we benefit from these insights and include them in the way we lead and manage in business?

In the early 1990s, we were missing the reasons for the varying levels of autonomy for successful cooperation in our productivity improvement projects. The iceberg in Figure 4 shows from top to bottom what our group went through.

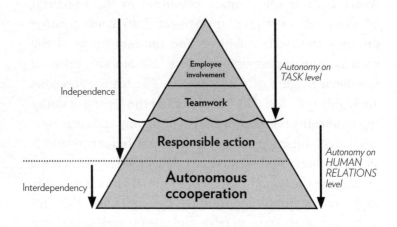

FIGURE 4

ORGANIZATIONAL AUTONOMY FOR COHESION AND COHERENCE

The adventure began with employee involvement. The popular saying then was that companies must draw from the intellectual power of all the workforce and employees should not be asked to leave their brains at home or in the locker room when coming to work. Everybody is independent and autonomous in their job and in their sphere of responsibilities, and everybody is required to participate in continuous improvement of their task and results. Organizations soon extended individual autonomy on task level to groups, once Kai-Zen, or its many derivations, was globally accepted and instructed. These management philosophies preach teamwork, where independent groups of people use their entire, available competencies and resources to achieve the company's mission and objectives together. A group turns into a team by building cohesion and many

fine models offer sensible recipes, e.g., 'Forming, Storm-
ing, Norming, Performing' (Tuckman, 1965). Teamwork is
a function of employee involvement, common team goals,
and objectives set and followed up by the hierarchy. Every
member covers his area of responsibility and delivery is
evaluated by management.

In entering the world below the water surface, one dis-
covers the base of the iceberg, out of sight to many and only
tangible to those who take the dive. Transcending to autonomy on the level of human relations is the crucial step to
a fundamentally different kind of operation. Here, performance of task completion is first and foremost a function
of the quality of human relations and when all other conditions are equal, this single change boosts performance of
the individual (responsible action) and the group (autonomous cooperation) to unbelievable heights. Autonomy at
the level of human relations refers to the free individual in
the unveiled state of mind and heart (Berne, 1963), allowing
for fulgurations and innovations, as well as for fruitful collaboration in a sound management environment. They are
the indispensable conditions and prerequisites for a team
to add interdependence to independence during its development to autonomous cooperation. Interdependency is
an essential driver in the journey to excellence and implies
high-performing human relations on a team, as described
in the American football example or the research of Michael
Tomasello. Autonomous cooperation is a crucial prerequisite for changing sustainably the Swiss way. In Swiss
democracy still today, autonomous cooperation allows the
different political parties to emerge and sustain cohesion
during difficult situations and in challenging decisions.

Big results come through teams and interdependency of teams is the fertile ground for change to emerge – innovations, new missions, objectives and tasks grow from any point in the organization and are exchanged, filtered and settled following the agreed-on rules. With hindsight, whenever autonomous cooperation was missing in our planned productivity improvements, results were not sustainable. Some projects established autonomous cooperation, some not, because we were letting high-performing human relations develop at random. On top, we were lacking a simple recipe. We left it to chance and, as such, results were often by chance. Certain persons are just 'naturals' in overcoming the barriers to autonomous cooperation, which in essence was the case wherever the changes in the projects were sustained. This sounds wonderful, of course, but the problem is there are just as many persons who are not so lucky, if not more. How do we help all groups reap the benefits of high-performing human relations for the whole organization?

As factory manager, I was asking this question, eager to install in the factory the kind of independence and interdependency cooperation flourishes on. Industry at the time was at its zenith of CI (Continuous Improvement) methodologies – Kai-Zen, TPM (Total Productive Maintenance), GMP (Good Manufacturing Practices) and SGA (Small-Group Activities) – and they were all great recipes for the journey to excellence. They were not totally new to us, as some had been around in the company for years already. Everybody was talking empowerment and so did we. The fashion was to empower the shop floor, but as leaders, we did not realize how much this would backfire. Empowerment by the leaders is unnecessary. People already have the power to act autonomously through their knowledge, experience and human genetics, and leaders have the obligation to grant the team the permission and protection to live this autonomy. Standing in front of a marathon runner and explaining how difficult marathons are and how much you need to distribute your strength, take care of hydration and energy intake, defeats the cause. You can practically hear the runner saying, "Please get out the way, so I can run my marathon." It dawned on us only much later.

We preached teamwork like everybody else. Team dynamics had long been a pivotal subject in management theories and teamwork a favourite. Most organizations then were satisfied with ensuring autonomy on the task level and proclaiming the independence of the employees. We wanted to go a step further, and that's why Madeleine Laugeri came on scene. She is a consultant for organizational improvement using Eric Berne's Theory of Organizations. Her consultancy had been recommended by the internal trainer from our local head office, a man I had deep respect for. What we did not know then was that her intervention would lead to our collaboration and mutual exchange for the next 20 years and finally to the development of the Emerging Change Model.

6

LEADERS AND PLANNED CHANGE

"When a group is in the 'here and now', it will develop its mutual expectations. Needs will emerge, evolve and be satisfied in a human process of continuous adjustment."

Madeleine Laugeri

We had just installed the third Nespresso production line which we had repatriated from Japan. Our objective was to export to Italy, home of the baristas, the country where espresso originally had been defined. The launch promised to be a special feat, comparable to the idea of importing Swiss cheese to Switzerland, and its success would confirm the superiority of the innovation. One could only imagine then the changes and their profound impact this little capsule would bring to the world of coffee for decades later. At the same time, we were industrializing an exciting new product targeting another consumer segment. Nobody before had shaped seven grams of roast and ground coffee in a perfectly round tablet, sealed between two layers of flexible foil and ready to use in a single-serve machine for delivering the perfect cup.

In our first meeting with Madeleine Laugeri, I explained the risks and opportunities we were facing in the factory. The consultant listened and, not surprisingly, asked the right questions. We were questioning the way most organizations were managing change, and she was ready to work together to find the answers, an opportunity worth taking. It was the mid-90s and the success of sharing my vision of people-centred management up to then had been very limited, for rarely had anybody given me the impression of understanding what my issue was; I was hesitating to hire an outside consultant for a subject so hard to explain. Multiple projects were running in parallel, and people felt the stress. More than 90% of production was exported, which suddenly was in danger as new trade barriers had become reality; consequently, the factory had to compensate by improving performance (cost, productivity and quality) to remain competitive and maintain production in Switzerland. This presented an intriguing task for the whole workforce; we had agreed to make the changes sustainably successful and avoid the risk of returning to square one, after all efforts were done.

The consultant proposed to experience daily life in our factory and join the team on a production line during its shift. I guess this convinced me to envisage collaboration. The factory had plans to offer a new SKU to a major customer from this line. One operator was running the filling machine in an air-conditioned room, a form/fill/seal filler for different pouch sizes and of German make. The filler was fed by a system run by another operator one floor above. A conveyer transported the filled pouches through an opening out of the filling room to the end of the line. They were grouped and a robot arm from a French manufacturer positioned them in a carton, which was glued and closed. Cartons were palletized by hand and brought to the warehouse by forklift. It was a simple set-up and line performance was low and unacceptable. The operators wanted to do a good job, but to them the machines were not reliable. When the German machine was working, the French equipment passed out and vice versa. The engineering and maintenance teams were ready to improve machine reliability but blamed the operators for their unskilled handling; we definitely needed to find a way to improve cooperation between operators and mechanics. Our answer was the promotion of a program called GMP (Good Manufacturing Practices) targeting a reduction of waste at the shop floor and adapted to our knowledge of Kai-Zen and TPM at the time.

We thought interdependence of the team members would result by explaining our common values and the required behaviours, and consequently allowing the production and maintenance people to improve together. This vision was shared in meetings with all employees in the green bean warehouse, surrounded by the odour of green beans in jute bags and where the experts presented piles of information, examples and figures on slides and posters. In essence, we were in good faith trying to instil the required behaviours for autonomy and cooperation from the top down.

Our plans for developing the right behaviours targeted the individual employees and included assessment procedures based on a company-wide evaluation scheme for measuring employee performance. It split individual performance into the 'what' and the 'how'. For evaluating the 'how', observed behaviours were rated based on an ingenious and near-to-perfect matrix describing the expected behaviours. After the manager had discussed the employee's improvement needs, action plans were agreed upon by both. Behaviours were measured by the hierarchy with the best of intentions, but autonomous cooperation in our teams was not really growing. Obviously, while we preached cooperation within a *team*, we were setting the wrong priorities by evaluating behaviours *individually*. There was a chapter in our appraisal scheme that covered cooperative behaviours; these were also assessed from the top down, which plainly defied its purpose, as we realized much later.

We believed our vision and plans had to be constantly reinfused by the hierarchy to have a chance to achieve the production objectives and the more we explained and planned for the people to work together, the less cooperation we saw. Later we installed BBS (Behaviour-Based Safety). The BBS system centres around a dialogue between an observer and a person being observed at their workplace. This was initially understood by the people as an audit, not really beneficial to establishing a climate of trust. Anybody in the organization could be the observer: a colleague, an employee from another department, a supervisor or the factory manager. The aim is to reduce accidents, which we actually did over time. A BBS dialogue coaches a person on a very specific behaviour observed with regard to occupational safety. It is successful when the coach (observer) is able to trigger the right feelings in the observed and, when done in an honest and trustworthy way, the people involved experience caring for each other, which obviously is a positive human relationship. When the emotional brain starts to think about occupational safety in a caring way, an improved safety behaviour has a good chance to emerge.

OHAS (Occupational Health and Safety) is undoubtedly a universal, common theme to mobilize emotional reasoning and create an environment of caring. Nobody wants accidents; we all want to be safe. The approach targeted the individual, which was all right, but it meant building and sustaining a network of individual dialogues addressing one person after the other – a huge undertaking for a workforce of hundreds of people. Caring for safety on an individual basis emerged, but we were not introducing caring *and* interdependency. Safety behaviours improved when the people were given the opportunity and the coaching to develop their own solution, but because we were not in dialogue with teams, our efforts did not yield the autonomous cooperation we were looking for. And still there was the odd area in the organization where safety dialogues were adopted by a team. These situations emerged when the whole group interacted in the 'here and now' and where the leader allowed the team a few minutes of their own, every shift, to exchange ideas. It was more the exception.

Attaining a change in behaviours seems obvious for an objective like safety; but how about cost reductions? Ambitious cost-reduction objectives can cause stress in the organization. We have all seen people fear losing their jobs and how cooperation then suffers. In these circumstances, instead of working on coherence and to stay on top of things and in control, leaders fall back to the style of reinforcing from the top down. This was what was happening on the filling line for pouches. It started at my level: the factory workers perceived the plans as orders from the top; as factory manager, I was giving the wrong signals when presenting and cascading the plans for improvement from the top down. We had our vision and common values, but the leadership team and I were not walking the talk ourselves; already the leadership team and I were missing a constructive dialogue. Middle management, the direct reports to the leadership team, were not very motivated to engage in cooperating autonomously in the change we had envisioned. They were not to blame, for how could they develop the required interdependency when the lack of cooperation was specifically evident at their bosses' level? We kept on planning continuous improvement through GMP even more meticulously and ever so much in detail, but without realizing that we were installing a sort of micromanagement. Freedom for autonomy was close to none, and people would just try to do the best they could to follow management's plan. It was *all* planned, and I was not yet aware of how counterproductive this was. Thus, improvements were never sustainable and they were at great cost. The targets for the pouch line had to be continuously readjusted downwards until we understood what a vicious cycle we were in and accepted that I was more the problem than the solution.

An excessive planning dynamic out of balance with emergence is a hindrance in an organization's journey to excellence, as shown by a famous Swiss example. In 2007, a federal councillor with an extraordinary political and industrial background was voted out of executive government against his will and the will of the leaders of his party, despite the fact that his political party was Switzerland's biggest and represented then nearly 30% of the voters. The episode was totally out of the norm. The Swiss public was split; some shouted scandal, others celebrated. What was going on?

Much analysis and documentation have commented on the reasons and rhymes of this unique incident. My interpretation is linked to the dynamic the resigning councillor had cultivated in the Swiss public for years, even before he had been elected to the Federal Council in 2003. It is what I call an excessive planned change dynamic. The councillor's plans were seen as imposing his political agenda on Switzerland, which was perceived as obstructing emergence and jeopardizing the Swiss way of high-performing human relations.

If a leader even at the helm of Switzerland, at the highest level of power, disregards the required balance of planned change and emergence, catalysed by a constructive dialogue as in changing sustainably the Swiss way, he will lose the trust and the confidence of the Swiss population and cooperation will suffer. This is exactly what happened. It is independent of the political programme of the person, for there will always be parts of the population that adhere to it, and others that disapprove of it. Diverging views of where the country is supposed to go and how it should get there is preferable; they are the necessary fuel for any democracy. It is also irrelevant to judge a person's behaviours as inadequate. The issue here is not of content or of convictions but of human relations and how they are central to consensus and cooperation for ensuring cohesion and coherence. In Switzerland, high-performing human relations are the condition *sine qua non* for the Swiss way of changing sustainably and putting them at stake is inadmissible. Coherence must be guaranteed by all means.

In this specific case, parliament rose in autonomous cooperation and while prioritizing coherence in the country prepared a plan and conducted its execution to remedy the situation and vote the councillor out of office. It amazed us all! Where does this power come from? It is rooted in the belief of our rituals and traditions, in the focused need for and the emergence of high-performing human relations for all in the management of Switzerland. Only by it will the country be on its journey to excellence in a process of changing sustainably the Swiss way.

So back in the factory, *I* had to change. I had to communicate my expectations clearly and directly with the leadership team, share my personal feelings about what was going on in the factory, show my true emotions and interact with my peers and direct reports constructively. I had to listen to the requirements of the leadership team, primarily, before reinforcing new missions and plans to the factory and, most important of all, I should never forget to give sincere signs of recognition. Simply put, I had to change my leadership style. Slowly the meaning of the phrase, "People do not care how much you know, if they do not know how much you care" dawned on me. Once we started this journey, the leadership team could work on their values and behaviours autonomously.

Up until then, my communication of vision and mission to the leadership team and the factory had been a one-way street. I was aware of employee involvement and engagement and the different continuous improvement approaches. We were all trained. But I was just planning their implementation and not living them myself. My plans were steamrolling over all efforts in the factory to foster autonomy and cooperation. The more I explained, the more elaborate the plans, the less our employees truly got engaged in autonomous cooperation. I believed we were installing the desired people-centred approach for improvement to reduce cost and become more competitive (our GMP project) and were mobilizing all employees; instead, we kept on force-feeding our plans and hindering autonomy from emerging. It was strange to change my style. I was asked to move from a top-down planning mode to letting the teams emerge with the right behaviours for cooperation, and this in a competitive environment, full of uncertainty and prospective failure; it sounded quite risky.

But when working with the leadership team on my demanded changes, a new process started in the factory: a human process. It awakened the kind of relationships we had been missing in our approach until then. There is a natural link between values and behaviours; it is human relations and when we interact we manage that link, which is what changing sustainably is about. When human relations are high performing, the desired cooperative behaviours emerge from trust and tolerance throughout the organization. The consultant coached us on analysing our situation and defining the essentials of the necessary change. We identified the classic dysfunctions:

- No constructive exchange in our weekly meetings; people do not speak up when they do not agree
- Meetings are too long and still there is never enough time; people are passive, mentally not present
- Context of the meetings is not clear to all participants.
- The leader is imposing his style, very authoritarian, not convincing
- The process is result-oriented only, not human-oriented.
- Lack of informal communication in the leadership team
- Lack of sharing who we are and what preoccupies us in our daily lives
- Lack of integrating newcomers
- The leadership team does not bring new subjects of concern to the meetings
- Too many meetings, no time to treat the unforeseen
- Too many projects, dilution of efforts and energy, deadlines not respected

What we wanted:

- The leader needs to address his concerns directly to the leadership *team* as a whole, as one body
- The leader needs to talk about himself: his feelings regarding the events in the factory, his personal values
- The leader needs to take initiative to integrate new-comers on the leadership team
- Previous work needs to be evaluated before asking for a new project
- The leadership team needs to participate in defining the agenda

We were making our first steps for a human process with emerging change, although we did not call it such then. We were trying things out and regularly reviewing the list of dysfunctions and needs. This alone resulted in the necessary traction for establishing a common definition and under-standing of our values and their desired expressions in our behaviours, yielding over time a new mode of management. It was not always clear to all why it worked, but over time we could experience growing autonomy and cooperation in the leadership team and the cascading of the human process into the factory. We were all excited to see us improve not only our behaviours but also our results: within three years our whole factory was considered competitive and capital investment projects of several hundreds of millions of CHF were attributed to the site. We did not fully grasp then the profound meaning of what was going on and what we had commenced. We had encountered the missing element for changing sustainably, which we had been searching for and did not realize it. We were not aware of this yet.

Today there is no question that high-performing teams are based on strong relationships – they are the bond between the organization's values and the teams' behaviours. But that is not enough. If leaders keep enforcing plans without a constructive dialogue, the teams lose confidence and autonomy and therefore cooperation and performance suffer. It is an issue in many current management approaches and implies an urgently needed evolution from leadership by top-down planning and objective management to a new style.

In *Team of Teams* (2015), Stanley McChrystal explains that teams are effective because members trust each other, have genuine relationships and a shared purpose. Leaders create 'shared consciousness' in their teams and the latter join up into networks. The leader cultivates an environment like a gardener, where every plant can grow simultaneously. The gardener metaphor comes close to the process thinking of TPM, where the 'farmer' prepares the ground on which improvements develop. He observes the environment and has the knowledge of the required methods and materials to facilitate progress. (In TPM, the 'farmer' interacts with the 'hunter' and the 'rock-blaster'. The 'hunter' seeks out new targets for becoming excellent. His work is complementary and synergistic to the farmer and their cooperation follows a continuous cycle. The 'rock-blaster' thinks and acts out of the box. From his search and research arise the innovational leaps, the seeds to be incorporated in the farmer's activity.)

The relationships among teams resemble the closeness among individuals of those teams. Each member is empowered to execute, as long as they provide all contextual information to leaders. McChrystal offers a list of tips for leaders on how to behave in meetings to foster trust, including creating a 'cheat sheet' with names, asking a question to show you listened, no need to give negative feedback to people, it can be done in private later, and don't pretend you know everything. All good as long as those leadership behaviours are humanly genuine.

In *Lessons from the Hanoi Hilton* (Fretwell & Kiland, 2013), the story of US Prisoners of War (POWs) in Vietnam traces how the POWs survived the atrocities of prison camp. Even in such inhuman circumstances, the moral frame and the power of human relationships acted as anchors for the imprisoned officers to endure their fate. The wisdom of how these prisoners managed is shared as fundamentals for building high-performing teams, e.g., the social network they established despite individual isolation and the 'we' thinking, leading to unconditional cooperation as a group.

In *Turn the Ship Around*, L.D. Marquet shows how he moved from a command-and-control style to leadership at every level with the leader-leader model for creating 'enduring excellence'. Leadership is not a cult and is decoupled from the leader's personality and presence. "Our greatest struggle is within ourselves. Old leadership of leader and followers is subconscious and one needs to clear one's mind of these preconceptions to see truly better ways for humans to interact" (Marquet, 2015).

Trust, the 'I intend to ...' principle, resistance to provide solutions by the leader and elimination of top-down monitoring systems are covered in the approach to attain the leader-leader model. Installing rituals supports the organization in managing change – for example, the use of the 'three-name-rule' (all soldiers greet every visitor using three names: the visitor's, the soldier's and the ship's) – it activates the emotional brain, which fosters pride in teams. Marquet asks, "Are your people trying to achieve excellence or just avoid mistakes? What is the primary motivation of middle managers? What we need is release and emancipation, fundamentally different from empowerment; with emancipation we are recognizing the inherent genius, energy and creativity in all people, allowing those talents to emerge. Have our processes become the master rather than the servant?" He continues demanding a space for open discussions within the teams, talking about their hunches and feelings where concerns are freely expressed, as well as ideas and hopes.

We take note of leadership styles in the army, which are in strong contrast to the command and control one would expect. In the examples mentioned, the intention to change originates from the leader. He is the boss and he creates. Hierarchy is not at all questioned. The officer stands above the soldier. The leader's knowledge is strategic, and he plans the overall change from the top. The teams are independent in execution; some decide on their strategic activities autonomously, some are described as clearly interdependent and Marquet even mentions how talents emerge through emancipation. Clearly the leaders are to be in balance between controlling the plan of activities and listening and responding to the requirements of the teams. These might seem unexpected premises for leading in the army; however, Marquet confirms how high-performing human relations are central to high-performing teams. But what happens when there is a new leader? How do teams guarantee their autonomous cooperation and continue emerging, and how sustainable is their human process? Marquet comes close to answering this in his book when he writes: "Only with this model can you achieve top performance and enduring excellence and development of additional leaders." The extraordinary success he has shown is highly impressive and deserves profound appreciation. Marquet later writes: "If the leader-leader model can work on board a nuclear submarine, it can work for you." This is what I question. Yes, it did seem to work fantastically on his ship, and I gladly subscribe to most of his insights and elements of his model. Nevertheless, experience has shown that leaders and teams must be in the 'here and now' for autonomous cooperation to persist, which is basically guaranteed on a submarine. It is inconceivable for a soldier to hide on a submarine when he is needed, a circumstance not always the case in all organizations, e.g., in a business cycle times can be so long and processes so complex it allows teams to detach from their strategic activities without it being immediately noticed. This is the reason many organizations need a structured process of changing sustainably, a human process that is complementary to and easily integrated into such models as referred to above.

In *From Leadership-as-Practice to Leaderful Practice* (2011), J. Raelin goes a step further. He defines a new leadership style: cocreation. He believes that a social organization should be developed collaboratively between its members through their free expression and shared engagement, democratic participation and leadership, including emotional and relational aspects. Raelin writes: "Leadership has to focus on social interactions and behavioural change within organizational life" (p. 2) and, "Leadership does not rely on the attributes of individuals, nor need it focus on the dyadic relationship between leader and followers" (p. 5). He continues: "At times when we are embedded in practice, we participate together in the collective emergence of ideas and actions heretofore unplanned and unadvocated" (p. 12) and, "Leadership becomes a social process that is as much lateral across a range of individuals connected with each other in practice as it is vertical from top managers to a cadre of followers" (p. 15). His thinking is fully in line with the definition of a human process with Emerging Change (Laugeri, 2015). As Raelin explains: "The vehicle to mobilize the democratic impulse is a genuine dialogue that has been depicted as an invitation for participants to a practice to co-create their socio-political consciousness." Not only does Raelin advocate autonomous cooperation, he also mentions that a planning dynamic is just another alternative to leadership as is the spontaneous and intuitive force of emergence.

TPM thinking echoes this wisdom: robustness before efficiency, experiment before plan and confidence before dogma, and in the Agile Manifesto we put individuals and interactions over processes and tools. But nowhere does Raelin, Agile nor TPM tell us how to do it. What unites the 'farmer', the 'hunter' and the 'rock-blaster'? How do we sustainably foster high-performing human interactions? Does the application and the implementation of TPM procedures in a team on a production line trigger high-performing human relations automatically? By now we know the answer is no. Leaders are required to rid themselves of their own barriers first and must understand and be aware of how to actively sponsor the implementation of sound human relations. Our experience in implementing TPM has confirmed this. When TPM activities and plans were pushed from the top down, the teams lost confidence and performance was not sustained. Successful AM (Autonomous Maintenance) teams strived to have a constructive dialogue in the team and with the hierarchy; they demonstrated ownership and engagement when trusted.

It is important for leadership to be built on trust and open dialogue. Social fairness, caring and sharing are neurobiological processes in human beings. Leaders must be aware of their emotional state and its impact, and they need to remove their own obstacles that hinder the natural deployment of these processes. Only then will high-performing human relations in our organizations have a chance to develop. These leaders plan long term, consider the strategic elements of the environment, and install and ensure the space for dialogue with the team. The new leaders let go of control, permit the team to emerge and foster autonomous cooperation. They will require courage and readiness to go with the flow of the team and even to accept failures. Not very easy to follow, especially in a competitive environment. So, the question remains: how to achieve this?

How does a middle manager, moving jobs frequently and constantly required to lead and follow in the journey to excellence, establish the virtuous circle for changing sustainably and ensure the required coherence for high performance? In our factory, we had continued learning for several years on how to improve our style and behaviours while installing our human process. By the time my successor took over, the values were embedded in the leadership team. The power of human relations fuelling the link to emerging behaviours was present. It was the leadership team that proposed to the incoming factory manager to continue the human process it had put in place.

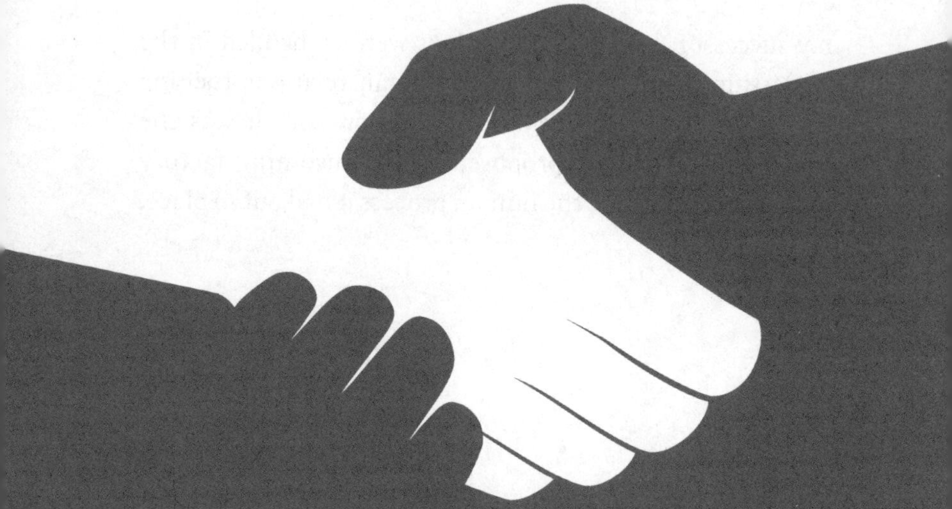

7

HUMAN
PROCESS
WITH
EMERGING
CHANGE

"**What strikes in emerging change is that it cannot be demanded or created. It is an energy, which generates its own development from the inside, independent of any external step.**"

Madeleine Laugeri

Early in the 2000s, I was assigned as technical director of our business in the south eastern region of Europe and became part of the management team reporting to the CEO of the region. My direct reports, the technical leadership team, were situated either in the factories of the region or at the head office. This technical leadership team followed a classical matrix structure: some members had direct operational responsibilities, while others were in charge of process expertise. They were peers, with senior levels of knowledge and skills, all seasoned and experienced employees, who had known each other and had worked together for years. The business results were good, the processes and systems robust but outdated, and we were in the middle of revamping them through a major global initiative of our company. Local leadership style was 'command and control' and also the members of the technical leadership team were used to having tasks delegated individually by the leader for their area of responsibility. The team, however, was not in autonomous cooperation and this became evident through the behaviours under stress or in crisis, in which circumstances, efficiency and effectiveness of human relations plunged and interactions at work turned into a massive drama. The team would then waste its time and energy in compensating for unsatisfying relationships by shouting or withdrawal, sometimes showing frustration or conflict, instead of focusing on the solution, and it was fully accepted; it was just the way they had been used to. It was their human process.

Many organizations have some kind of human process, which is structured around people's behaviours, values and human relationships. A sample human process is described in the book *Leadership and Self-Deception: Getting Out of the Box*

(The Arbinger Institute, 2009). It refers to a common human behaviour: we tend to judge others before we view ourselves, and this is defined as self-imposed ignorance or being in a box. The advocated human process in this example is getting out of the box, a human process where human relations are built on 'ok-ness'. The book describes that people are ok by default and should be treated correctly; behaviours are not the target in itself, but a function of the feelings and relationships. People should be trusted and confidence not automatically withdrawn in case of mistakes. To achieve such practice, a leader needs first to question himself before he questions others and treat people like he would want to be treated. The authors call it getting out of the box. The rules and the principle of getting out of the box are transmitted to the newcomers through conversations with the leaders. The CEO takes on the process which is then propagated throughout the company by the principle of following the leader. Such a human process is definitely an excellent step to improve human relations, and the authors confirm the clear link between its implementation and improved performance of the organization; truly, having everybody in an organization live such an ideal is a wonderful achievement.

We were looking for 'ok-ness', but in a human process with an additional dynamic. What we see in the example above is improved caring based on a dialogue between individuals. We wanted caring and *emergence* in teams, and we were searching for a human process that manages the relationships not only on an individual basis, but between the leader and the team *as a whole*, and between each of the members of the team.

Human processes are, in many instances, insufficiently taken care of, awareness is low and little investment attributed. Why is that? Human relations belong to the soft side of management, are not measurable and therefore thought to be intangible and too complicated to be managed appropriately. Many companies are of the opinion that it would be even a contradiction to use the word 'human' with the word 'process'. I beg to differ. Our reasoning consciously or unconsciously is clearly linked to neurobiological *processes* unfolding in the human brain. For me, it is a crime not to adequately identify and properly manage the human process of any group. Some of the highest returns on investment organizations of our current times can reap from are in a human process for rendering emergence.

A human process with emergence managed proactively by all leaders and teams of an organization should be high on the agenda of any business on its journey to excellence. Ignorance or sloppiness in addressing relationships can quickly make them a limiting factor for improving an organization's results. Successful management of an organization's human process deserves at least the same attention as technical and business processes or as the management of knowledge and skills. I am referring here to the existence of three distinct dynamics on the journey to excellence, as shown in Figure 5 on p. 120.

How knowledge, technical and human processes interplay, the Swiss way, can be shown in the example of the Swiss apprenticeships system. Apprenticeships are very highly respected in Switzerland and rightly so. They are an important and significant cornerstone of the Swiss economy and society; many of the successful leaders in business and politics started their careers after grade school as an apprentice. The Swiss way of apprenticeships comprises three or four years of training and education in real time. Youngsters are integrated into work life, where they need to live cooperation and learn by doing. The apprentices start with the basics of their trade in the actual daily social and economic surroundings and activities of a company. The practical and human experience, the trade knowledge and the technical expertise gained are invaluable in understanding the work, the workers and the social and economic life in our country and a perfect start for the individual into the world of outstanding craftmanship or of later schooling in college or university. Acquiring the notions and importance of all three vectors – the human, the technical and the knowledge – at young age is an excellent preparation for understanding the requirements of and for integrating into our direct democratic society. It becomes a way of living, the Swiss way.

Groups should manage these three vectors in equilibrium or they will waste their time and effort and penalize their overall performance. Best of all, as human beings we are predestined and carry around with us all that is needed to invest in a high-performing human process and get lots of return; we just need to apply it. Corporations spend tons of money and tremendous efforts in managing their technical processes and business systems or on training and competency building. Nobody questions this and rightly so, but for the human process, a little a day goes a long way.

We might find our modern technocracy exaggerated and, with reference to the size of some of the IT departments one encounters, it could seem that things are out of balance.

Let's, however, remember that engineers, technical experts, scientists and the workforces in factories, R+D and operations design, develop and run our technical processes, producing the goods and services that are the foundation of our prosperity; efficient technical processes are essential for our survival. The requirements of humanity, now and in the future, will be met by sustainable technical processes, knowledge and expertise. There is no doubt, however, and also a disturbing trend, to this truth: becoming an engineer or a technical expert today is not as attractive anymore in our society. Firms recruiting are not as vocal for engaging the technical graduates' interests and often, straight out of school, they start at a lower salary level than their marketing or finance colleagues. Engineers are often made responsible in public, supported by the media, for the many problems of our progress today, such as the developments that are leading to pollution, resource depletion or even global warming. This sounds strange, for is it not primarily ignorance and insufficient interest in the consequences of exploiting those processes for short-term benefits instead of keeping them in balance for the long-term that is the issue? And on top we see whole nations vote for and install leaders who seem to disregard the importance of technical understanding. Leaders and key decision makers should seek to acquire the necessary knowledge and be sufficiently informed of the big picture painted by the technical processes in the long run, a priority that should stand above marketing the short-term results.

In Johan Wolfgang v. Goethe's renowned tale of the sorcerer's apprentice, 'Der Zauberlehrling' (Goethe, 1798), reminds us, in an unmistakable way, of what happens when the need for comprehension of technics is underestimated and how things can go wrong when our emotions are in disequilibrium with our technical knowledge. The master sorcerer leaves the apprentice alone at home to perform his chores, including the cleaning of the floor with a broom and a bucket. The apprentice, not too excited about the physical effort and overrating his own capabilities, plays it smart and while using his master's magic, enchants the broom to perform the job. He does not fully comprehend the applied witchery and very quickly has to watch things get out of hand: the broom grabs the bucket, runs to the fountain, speeds back to the magician's atelier and instead of wiping and mopping, spills the water over the floor, then heads off again to fetch more. Within no time the room is flooded and the apprentice up to his ankles. Obviously, he lacks the knowledge to stop the broom from hauling pail after pail and, in desperation, takes to an axe leaning by the woodstove. With one blow he splits the broom in two. Unfortunately, each part now becomes a whole new broom and the process continues at twice the speed, creating double the mess. The brooms stop and the story ends when the sorcerer returns and breaks the spell, bringing the errand process finally to a halt.

When observing the recent developments of polarization, oppositions and disrupted partnerships in our modern socio-economical world, it seems legitimate to ask if our objectives and our needs are in coherence. Without coherence, any organization is doomed and sometimes we wonder who will stop those enchanted brooms. The assumption here is that the human process with emerging change enables people, leaders and teams to establish coherence in their organization. The question has been posed, are homo sapiens capable of such a feat? I think yes. Darwin had been looking for the missing link and some say it is us. Are we just an intermediary step? When listening to evolutionary biologists and by contemplating our own limitations and the global challenges we are confronted with, we can easily believe so and we could feel discouraged; we can, however, also imagine the forces of evolution, of changing sustainably with emergence of which we ourselves are a product, to continue its proven course and the populations in our world to emerge in groups, in our *cultural* evolution, not by mutation and selection, but rather by applying a human process with emerging change. This will allow for all to work together in our quest for excellence. Yes, such statements may sound utopic' and naive and we know of the countless, huge obstacles to overcome. I believe it is worth more than a try, at least in business for starters; the venture takes little effort, close to no investment and the chances of success are substantial as emerging change does not reinvent but builds on our natural dispositions to respond to our feelings and needs for sane and satisfying human relations. It all begins with awareness. It works in Switzerland. When leaders understand emergence and have experienced its power and massive benefits to organizations, then applying this framework becomes simple and quickly sustainable.

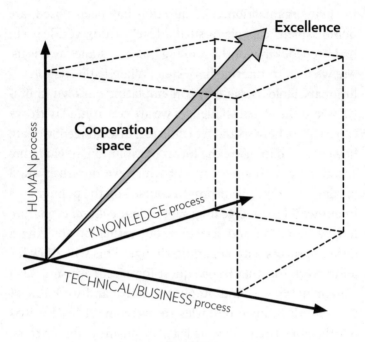

FIGURE 5

THE JOURNEY TO EXCELLENCE

A human process with emerging change is applied independently of the organization's culture, structure, nature of objectives or specific environment. A human process with emerging change and its three contracts successfully unfolds through the efforts of leaders and teams to keep the following elements in equilibrium:

- A vision contract expressing the desire to live a structured and conscious approach of drawing from the totality of the potential of all people for business, continuous, cultural or any other excellence

- The power of using the emotional brain as a fully accepted partner to rationality within our moral frames
- The requirements of coherence between the people (the teams) and the objectives of the organization
- A leader's mission contract for giving space to and dialoguing constructively with the team and enabling change to emerge
- A cooperation contract facilitating autonomous cooperation and creating interdependency
- Emergence in teams through their mission contract with the leader
- The rituals of promoting continuous improvement of human relations in partnership and making changing sustainable

Emerging change can be integrated into any management model, old or new. Many new-wave approaches – such as 'self-organizing teams', 'l'entreprise libérée' and 'agile' or 'holocracy', just to name a few – are referring to emergence, rituals, emotions and relationships in teams and with leaders. A human process with emerging change is the simple and efficient response to these references and supports the implementation of those and many other models.

Years before in the factory, we had made it clear how we needed to focus and improve our human process. We were investing in the three vectors and still our efforts had been insufficient and rendered the management of our values and behaviours incomplete – we had been focusing on individuals and not on teams. A human process is, then, of most advantage when applied on the team level, as in emerging change, and this was the test for my new assignment as technical director. Our human process had to ensure sustainability of the changing process installed and the results achieved by the team as a whole. Experience had shown that it was not enough to explain and prescribe the integration of our values and the desired behaviours; instead, we now intended to achieve high-performing human relations for the people to live those values and behaviours as a team and this was first priority, for only then would we reach autonomous cooperation and the conditions for emergence.

We proposed to introduce the human process with emerging change (although we did not call it such yet) as part of our company-wide project for the preparation and installation of our new technical and business processes. The team said yes right from the start, not fully convinced perhaps, but eager to try it nonetheless. After initial individual interviews by the consultant, we planned a two-day workshop applying 'hot chair' and 'mirror chair' (Laugeri, 2015). In our workshop we kicked off the plan and created awareness for the necessary autonomy in the team's relations, issuing and sharing with the leadership team the first version of the vision contract. In our mission, we were asking to install autonomous cooperation and align on how we wanted to work as team and leader. This resulted in regular reviews of our contracting and adjustments of the gaps in our relationships, each time rendering our exchanges for defining and agreeing on our requirements of collaboration more efficient, ambitious and professional. We were creating powerful and high-performing human relations where our relational needs were met, while we achieved our objectives. It all sounded pretty fuzzy in the beginning, but became an integral part of how we interacted over time. In line with the mission, the team installed an impressive cooperation contract: the leadership team suggested defining its ten most important behaviours for autonomous cooperation and measuring them on a regular basis. It resulted in a totally different outcome than what I had experienced, where behaviours were assessed by hierarchy. Everybody reviewed everybody else on each of the chosen ten common behaviours and gave them a score from one to ten, ten being excellent. The data was graphically represented and was shared and discussed in the team. As leader, I was not involved and not meant to be either; however, the team gave me the opportunity to see the results.

Behaviours on the team measured by the team can be so powerful that improvements are nearly immediate, if its human relations are sound (if not, it can create even more problems and team members can actually regress). In our case, the team had known each other for a long time, which helped. Their relations at work, although not high performing, were built on 'ok-ness'. Obviously, there were conflicts, but we were lucky enough to have the one team member who quickly grasped the benefits of cooperation and acted as coach and this, together with the consultant's support, strongly facilitated the process. Through the behaviour measures, the leadership team directly identified where as individuals they were appreciated on the team and where they were lagging. Improvements emerged and were close to instant.

The team was proud to have installed a human process that guaranteed coherence of their needs, activities and objectives. A human process with emerging change is a two-way street: teams have the obligation to cooperate autonomously, support and help their peers (at the time we called it the green or bottom-up dynamic) and their leaders (the red or top-down dynamic) manage the strategic elements of the environment and collaborate in a space of constructive dialogue with the team. For us, both dynamics were in harmony for creating the necessary high-performing human relations and, in the years to follow, we had several fundamental changes in how the technical team managed to achieve the targets. Stress became manageable and focus was now on the output and not on the drama. Emerging change did not modify the team's way of showing emotions in their interactions. When applying emerging change, people will still be who they are, true to their culture. However, emerging change took out some of the pain and the waste in the teams' relations and, as a result, cooperation became speedy and agile. This new cooperation simplified peoples' lives, not only professionally, but in some cases personally as well. One senior manager on the leadership team admitted that even his wife had remarked on the change in him. The impact was obvious. The team's results were remarkable with over-expected growth in the most profitable areas, and when one factory had to be closed and another divested, it happened in the frame of trust and tolerance and with compassion, addressing and covering the needs of the employees and respecting the objectives of the businesses.

A human process with emerging change makes teams and leaders evolve from routines to rituals, from human resources to human relations and from engagement to emergence. This makes life easier and can, as in our case, improve results.

THE
MODEL OF
EMERGING
CHANGE

"Things would have been different had I lived somewhere else. The Swiss efficient and peaceful democracy has inspired many aspects of the emerging change methodology."

Madeleine Laugeri

Emerging change sustainably makes a group realize the most unusual and unforeseen products for satisfying customers, consumers and employees while simplifying structures and minimizing cost for more output. When a team emerges, it communicates its needs and its proposals as one entity and with one voice for reaching the organization's objectives in the most efficient and effective manner. This is a fundamental dynamic of changing sustainably the Swiss way and is still today the agreed-upon manner in which in the Swiss executive government operates throughout all its ranks.

Organizations turn flexible with emerging change; they can respond directly and continuously to the requirements internally and to the opportunities externally once the people's interest in identifying the relational needs of the group is established. The heartbeat of excellence lies in the Swiss way of changing sustainably and emerging change is its lifeblood. It is the heart with the force to throb for the long necessary changes in our global socio-economic and political landscapes bringing cooperation and coherence to life.

The innovational leap lies in proposing a simple and universal approach to a seemingly complex process of managing human relations and the concept is of very easy use; it relates to the traditional and general wisdom that a good relationship to the parent demands a good relationship between siblings. The functioning of emerging change can be explained in a few minutes and during the first coaching sessions, the process immediately creates powerful insights for leaders and teams.

The Model of Emerging Change is described in Madeleine Laugeri's *Les Clés du Dialogue Hiérarchique* (*The Keys to the Hierarchical Dialogue*). Laugeri reduces the variety and complexity of many management approaches to a single common point – human relations. In any organization and independent of the advocated leadership styles, hierarchy or self-organizing teams, groups of people or individuals, the common denominator is the dynamics of how human beings relate to one other. This is not surprising, but perhaps what is astonishing is the little care we give to this fact in business and the minimal effort we exert when it comes to managing human relations for the benefit of the organization's results. Emerging change is the model for turning this simple truth of one unique common driver – human relations – into a competitive edge for all businesses and a key success factor for the organization.

The time is ripe. The younger generations, Generations Y and Z, are coming to work today, openly asking for this change to happen. Emerging change is a systemic approach, which allows an organization to stay fit and develop its activities in a healthy manner, through their permanent adjustment to the changing demands of the external world and ensures, in analogy to our evolution, survival and promotion of the organization. Teams applying emerging change will anticipate and fulfil rapidly and efficiently the requirements of the market, because every team takes responsibility for its actions.

Emerging change, generally speaking, is a series of conversations taking place between leaders and teams and within teams. The model establishes the frame for the implementation and maintenance of these conversations, which develop to constructive dialogues. There are three main types of dialogues in the human process of an organization (Laugeri, 2015). These dialogues take place across the three organizational boundaries as previously discussed in Chapter 5 and they are established between people, when different characteristics, belongings or opinions are felt. Laugeri calls these dialogues contracts because it reflects the shared expectations and needs, the awareness and commitments on each side of the human boundaries. The nature and quality of the contracts play an important role in the quality of work life and for producing the organizational results, whether or not the boundaries are consciously formalized or recognized. Contract in this instance does not refer to a document, and it is not an official agreement. Contracting occurs on a regular basis and is formalized and maintained under conditions called ritual meetings. Contracts install bridges across boundaries and adjust the different forces exerted by leaders and teams; they help regulate the stroke economy from scarcity to abundance (Steiner, 2009).

Figure 6 shows the three different contracts:

- Vision contract
- Mission contract
- Cooperation contract

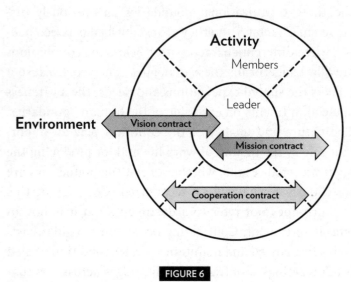

FIGURE 6

THE THREE CONTRACTS OF EMERGING CHANGE

People focus on a mutual exchange of recognition, information and proposals through contracting, with the purpose of imago adjustment (exchange of up-to-date information about the group), rather than committing to an improvement or result. Being informed of each other's needs and requests is enough for people to do their best at work; pressing forward for commitment is unnecessary and pushes people into reactions of over-adapted or rebellious behaviour, rendering the team inefficient and prone to psychological games. Teams and leaders anticipate and can prevent part of the gaming by creating a 'stroke economy' that feeds them with authentic recognition (strokes).

VISION CONTRACT

"The vison contract is the leader's privilege." Madeleine Laugeri

The vision contract helps the leader deal with the pressure from the environment. It belongs to the leader exclusively and covers the collection of input for developing the team's objectives.

The leader:

- identifies and prioritizes the strategic elements of the environment external to the group which are essential for its success
- develops the vision and the objectives and shares them externally and internally with the group in ritualized meetings
- positions his organization socially to ensure appropriate visibility and success in dealing with all the external parameters that influence the survival of the organization

In the vision contract, the leader expresses his desire to work in partnership with the team.

MISSION CONTRACT: TEAM AND LEADER AT THE MAJOR INTERNAL BOUNDARY

The mission contract clarifies the terms and conditions of a continuous and constructive dialogue between the team and the leader with the sole purpose to position the team as an ok+ partner (Laugeri, 2015). All other technical and business matters need to be addressed in other exchanges.

The mission contract consists of two parts, mission contract A and contract B. In the mission contract A the leader asks the team to develop and prepare their mission B and cooperation contracts. He grants adequate time and space for this purpose.

The ritual of the **mission contract A** consists of the leader:
- thanking the team and sharing what is appreciated
- informing the team of what the needs are in their dialogue
- deciding on the proposals made by the team

The ritual of the **mission contract B** involves the team:
- thanking the leader and sharing what is appreciated
- informing of what its needs are in its dialogue with the leader
- proposing an implementation strategy and a task distribution

In preparation of a mission contract B, the team shares internally what is strategic in its activities to guarantee the achievement of the overall objectives of the organization. The team then prioritizes its strategic elements and develops task proposals based on its agreed-upon way of decision-making. In this contract, the team establishes a win/win relationship with the leader and is empowered to emerge with its contribution to the objectives (task distribution and strategic activities) reflecting an unscripted reality of the activity status (Berne, 1963). This exchange is continued until both parties are in a satisfactory dialogue, which the team and the leader will need to practice and further develop according to their evolving demands. Through the mission contracts A and B, leadership and team members become credible partners. Mission contracting is not a forum for discussion and should be brief, at most a half hour; it takes place in a welcoming and comfortable place. The group determines who speaks first. The leader, if proposed to start, reads his own text listing the different elements of the mission contract A. The team thanks the leader and takes time to ask comprehension questions only. Then each member of the team, in turn, will read one item of the list of its mission contract B. The leader thanks the team and takes time to ask his comprehension questions. There is no space for comments at this stage other than gratitude. Nobody has to formally commit to anything. The meeting concludes with a roundtable, where each participant shares what moved him and how he felt during the dialogue. The team should work first on its cooperation contract, to issue a relevant and effective mission B and perform a satisfactory contracting dialogue.

COOPERATION CONTRACT

"The cooperation contract implies that team members consider their feelings and what is going on in their work life as strategic information and their relationships with peers a priority – even over their own subordinate team." Madeleine Laugeri

The cooperation contract is the team's privilege. The team identifies and prioritizes the relevant strategic elements of their activity in consensus. Having the whole team present is best, definitely in the beginning; however, it not necessarily indispensable as the contract evolves. It is better not to postpone a meeting due to the absence of some members. Just as individuals may not feel responsible for what is going on in their lives and impute things to chance, some teams do not know who they are and do not seem to be aware of what is strategic in their contribution to the success of the organization. They do not deal with their daily issues by themselves and place unrealistic expectations on their leaders or their environment to prevent or solve their problems. They are not in autonomous cooperation. Yet, as there are strategic elements of the environment considered in the vision contract, there are also strategic elements of the activity. The latter are elements of the 'here and now', e.g., the external and internal circumstances within the department, the events (absences, conflicts), the competencies in the organization, the breakdowns of machines, the substandard deliveries from suppliers or to customers; in principle, all the elements that condition the success of the daily tasks. The more team members inform each other about their personalities and their systems (how they tick) in their professional fields, the better they will manage these elements of activity.

Not all are visible to the manager, so their importance tends to be discounted by the team members. On top, most people will mind their own business and not see the necessity to share, often thinking it is a waste of time and an interdiction to interfere with the responsibilities of their colleagues, a belief many times reinforced by the management style of their boss. The team members, when sharing the strategic elements of their own segment, develop personally and create the team identity. The cooperation contract empowers the team as a whole to take its responsibility for achieving an ok+/ok+ partnership with the leader and for solving the problems that can be treated at its level. The team can create its cooperation contract *only in the absence of the leader*, a fact still not respected in many current management philosophies. In the ritual of cooperation contracting, the team members:

- greet and thank each other and share what is appreciated in their professional interactions
- inform each other of what goes well and what difficulties each member has in dealing with his own segment of activity, expressing the needs and requests for support in the strategic elements of their activity
- prioritize the shared information with the aim of dealing with the issues in the team and to prepare for escalating remarks, proposals and requests to the leader as one voice

When a team works this way, only relevant, authentic information reaches the leader. There is no manipulation into decisions. The leader is not torn between different opinions or options, proposed by competing team members.

The leader gets the right and true information about the structure potential in the 'here and now' and is informed of what he needs to know about the strategic elements of the activity.

At the individual level, the cooperation contract requires a high degree of autonomy: ability to trust, confidence in one's own competence and pride in the competence of peers, sharing of vulnerabilities and the pleasure of doing common work. The cooperation contract is the preparation for the mission contract B and gives a group of peers reason and responsibility to develop personally and establish the image of the team they want to be.

Installing the three contracts of emerging change means:

- for the leader: relief of stress and guilt of having to make difficult decisions alone, when there is no crisis, development of trusting the team as a reliable and ok+ partner, installation of the communication channel to the team as a whole and permission for personal request and intimacy
- for the team: every person and every personal experience has value and sharing those, in appropriate settings, is a precious gift to the community and may result in unforeseeable benefits to the organization by emergence. Discounting this would mean discounting the willingness of peers to receive strokes and develop priorities to be communicated to the leader. It may also discount the leader's positive intentions to acknowledge and decide upon the team's message

The three contracts, when fully embedded in the way teams and leaders exchange, are the organization's recipe for emergence and subsequently for changing sustainably in organizational life. Installing emerging change in any journey to excellence means innovating proactively and responding to specific needs of an organization, e.g., structure change, arrival of a new leader or team member, anticipation of crisis, conflict management, regulation of workload or cost control.

9

APPLYING
THE THREE
CONTRACTS

"Cooperation and mission contracts can be seen as joint definitions of responsibilities and expected behaviours."

Madeleine Laugeri

Changing sustainably the Swiss way is founded on the constant interaction of the forces of planned change exerted by the leadership and of emergence created by the group membership. It unfolds by seeking an equilibrium of these energies through continuous, constructive dialogue between leaders and teams. In the absence of this dialogue or in the instance of excessive planned change by the leader, things get out of balance and emergence remains unfulfilled.

The latter was the main reason why later our continuous efforts of applying a human process with emerging change throughout my various positions as technical director led to varying results. Some teams emerged, while some did not at all. We tried to involve peers, leverage autonomous cooperation and emerge as a team for boosting our performance. We were struggling.

In an environment of excessive planned change, e.g., disproportionate control of the people's activities that can induce disrespect of the major internal boundaries by the leader, seeking permission and protection from the leader to focus on a human process with emerging change is a challenge. When the dynamics of planned change in a group are lacking vision and mission contracts, the seeds of emergence have little chance to germinate; excessive planned change kills emergence. It is not necessarily the leadership style of command and control that is the cause. Autonomy on task level may still be expected by the manager but when trust and tolerance are missing, a human process with emergence will have no chance. Leaders should be aware of their crucial role in initiating the process of changing sustainably the Swiss way. They must go through an emotional process to establish 'ok-ness' and partnership with the team.

If this does not happen, they run the risk of reinforcing their own planned change with all good intentions and the team will not develop the necessary autonomous cooperation and resulting coherence sustainably. Consequently, the individuals may seek to withdraw or pass their time other than in the needed mutual activities to achieve the objectives.

The management meetings in my next position as head of an R+D (Research and Development) centre were exciting and great fun, seldom with open conflicts. Once a week the leadership team, all direct reports, department heads and staff, stood in front of our continuous improvement board. It was bolted to a wall in the corridor on the first floor, a busy place where the main traffic of employees and visitors passed by. We were close to a dozen people. We lacked space around the board and whoever was in the back had to stretch and get on his toes when it came to following figures and graphs. Participation was phenomenal; everybody had something to share, often joking and laughing, but our relations were superficial with little intimacy. Basically, we were wasting our time.

In such a situation, the one individual is not really interested in what the other thinks, feels or says. Everybody has already a lot on their plate and one can live very well without additional preoccupations from other departments: "Why should I be concerned about my colleague's troubles and successes?" Delegation of tasks to such a group as a whole then triggers endless discussions, teamwork is not really existent and the leader thinks he must carry it all on his own shoulders. Work is performed in silos; improving interaction or even creating interdependency between departments is not on the agenda at all. Managers look after themselves and their own reports, mind their own business and question what they have in common with other departments and why they should change. What a huge potential for improvement.

J.A. Raelin states: "Clearly, if we are interested in developing leadership along practice and leaderful lines (everyone is participating in the leadership of the entity both collectively and concurrently), leadership development will require a different approach from the more classroom epistemology that pulls managers out of their workplace to attend classes that presume to teach leadership competencies. It makes little sense indeed to teach leadership to individuals in a public setting detached from the very site where leadership is occurring." So the last thing you want to do is to send your leaders again to a business or management school or hold lectures on leadership in a classroom. In our case, we did leave the office for the odd internal seminar or spend an evening together over a 'cook your own' dinner or at a sports event. We had fun and generated a small and fragile sort of intimacy, but it quickly became clear that this alone would not improve our objectives at work.

The strategic environment had changed and there were new objectives in the pipeline. Top-down targets asked for higher performance through improvements of efficiency *and* the quality of our output. In our management discussions, we expressed the wish to install changes as a team without rocking the boat, but by powering the organization instead; the leadership team was competent and capable of making the difference successfully, not as individuals but in cooperation. Nobody questioned this openly, but after our weekly meetings, the department heads would vanish and go back to their sections. We needed a vision contract.

I invited Madeleine Laugeri to visit us. It took a few weeks until she had interviewed the whole leadership team, and I did not see the results, for it was her and only her diagnostic to support us in the installation of the three contracts. In the beginning, suspicion was in the air – an external consultant, what did she want? The belief was that things were going well, there was a new leader with a strange vision about changing sustainably but no crisis or sign of one; over time, however, her assistance started to be appreciated by the team. We had no desire to invent a burning platform, advice given by leading gurus in managing change. Rather, I shared with the leadership team what I was expecting: we, the team and I, were to work as partners. The department heads had to stop viewing the head of the centre as the absolute authority of judgment, where all major decisions and supporting signatures had to pass through. We had to start working on our relationships and on the space for a continuous constructive dialogue. In this context, each one needed to develop his individual autonomy for responsible action. Only then would the individuals be open to helping each other and ready to exchange in their activities.

The leader must make clear that he is willing to support such a change with whatever it would require. This new approach means reviewing and clarifying roles of leader and leadership team. For the leader, it is a big step. It implies primarily to let go and allow the team business time on their own, a question of trust and tolerance. Teams may accept with open arms! On the other hand, team members can react vehemently; they will feel awkward or see uncertainty and instability in this manner. A leadership team has to live up to its name and take leadership as a team, not as individual department heads. An organization cannot be satisfied by breaking down its objectives into personal targets. This point of view can be a novelty and spread even more discomfort. Nevertheless, establishing the space for a team to interact at work without the leader means planting the seeds of trust and tolerance. It is decisive for the leader to hand out signs of recognition, putting emphasis on the appreciation of the team's willingness to cooperate in the leader's absence.

During presentations in our regular operations meetings, I stepped back or out of the room. It was a shock in the beginning and, although I had originally shared my intentions, some would look over their shoulders, unsure of what was going on, or just stop and await my return, asking why I had abandoned them. When I joined the wrap-ups, I recognized the team's efforts of becoming autonomous, which I prioritized over the content of the team's discussions. This will surprise but gets the message across.

Over time we initiated 'meteo', an adjustment of imago (Berne, 1963). 'Meteo' is a group's small, daily experience of daring, sharing and caring where on top of the agenda stands the question: "What's the weather like today inside?" Participants are asked to take turns in sharing very briefly the feeling and/or preoccupation they are momentarily carrying around. The whole round for everybody to speak up takes only a few minutes, because during 'meteo' the audience is supposed to listen without commenting to the one participant speaking. The group then rewards immediately with an unconditional, personal thank you.

In the beginning, the team members did not speak up; some would lower their gaze, staring at their hands on the table, clearly preventing eye contact, and others would cast glances of disbelief in their surroundings or not talk at all. This was all fine, as it was essential not to force anyone. If a team had been used to judgment in the past, then positive unconditional signs of recognition from the boss represent an absolute novelty; the leader finally establishes the necessary hierarchical permission to play by following the new ritual consistently himself.

"In an environment of increasing demands at work, we cannot underestimate the impact that the sharing of the strategic elements of the activities of the team has and the substantial human warmth it generates. The feeling of individual stress and incapacity is replaced by a powerful source of stimulation and recognition," says Madeleine Laugeri. Suddenly we sensed we were in the same boat, if only for a few minutes. Team members would discharge and, while connecting the dots, recognize their communalities.

In spite of the advancements in the awareness of our relationships, there was still little readiness from the team to help each other in the day-to-day interactions outside the meetings and not much agreement on how crucial it was for the centre's success. My talks of how we would work together and how we would manage the requirements of the team as partners, while reaching the objectives of our mission, were accepted but not convincing. It seemed impossible to explain. Once the leader explains he is in the planning dynamic, this carries the risk of the team withdrawing if the contracts are not in place, which was our case.

An organization needs to align on the significance of its internal boundaries for preparing the contracts. Organizations constantly bump into the same issue. Is the leader part of the leadership team? In emerging change, leaders are not part of, they are in *partnership with* the leadership team. The leader is part of another team, together with his or her peers. When the leader realizes this, stops controlling all the details and fights off the desire of constant physical and mental presence, the risk of excessive planned change is reduced. If managers are used to 'helping' make the major decisions for the daily operations, sometimes with and many times for their direct reports, then the direct reports can have a hard time understanding that they need to work together on the organization's issues in cooperation without the leader. In a successful leadership team, members go first to their peers and not to the boss with their problems and questions for reaching the group's objectives. Understanding then the psychological play of the major and minor internal boundaries (Figure 3) must be high on the agenda.

For moving forward at the centre, we had to start in a favourable spot. The financial and people impact of the new objectives made the head of finance and control, together with the head of human resources, spontaneously take the lead and propose a plan for communication. It was enough for the whole team to engage in an involved discussion without me; it was the first step in the direction of our vision contract. To issue the vision contract, I had to review the major internal and external strategic elements for the centre with my boss, our customers, business partners and suppliers. The main obstacle was to show feasibility of improving output while simultaneously producing cost savings. Rationally everybody can grasp this; emotionally it stays an act of defiance, and to move forward we required input, agreements and buy-in from the business units and the R+D community. Tough objectives can raise questions in people. There might not be visible rebellion, but without a cooperation contract, people might silently hope the cost reductions will hit some other unit.

The vision contract of the leader is best achieved when he is in cooperation with his peers; it catalyses the team's own cooperation. Fortunately, the R+D coordinator in the major business unit and I were on the same page; through our mutual respect, we were able to settle on the necessary support and agreements for the centre's vision contract, including how we wanted to cooperate as a business unit and R+D. We did not issue a written cooperation contract, but our relations were sound. We were in a series of constructive dialogues that represented a crucial first step in convincing the leadership team at the centre and getting it on board. Once the vision contract was formalized, we installed the space for review in our regular management meetings.

The next step was the mission contract A to the leadership team. My first version included the centre's targets and plan of achievement; after all, we were referring to the mission of the centre. It did not work, and we were losing too much time focusing on figures, bogged down on details. In the second issue of my mission contract A, I voiced my expectations solely on managing our relationships and presented it to the whole team in our designated contracting time during our weekly meeting. My requirements for the team were:

1. Speaks up when they do not understand
2. Installs a cooperation contract
3. Shows solutions to achieve the targets
4. Respects the timing and agenda of our meetings
5. Shares how they want to be rewarded
6. Tells me what to follow up on my weaknesses

It only took 15 minutes and triggered small response, with the rare request for more clarification. Generally speaking, the points in the first mission contract A are of such nature that there is little room for argument, for human relational needs become evident once you voice them. But this is not enough for a team to emerge. I was wishing for the leadership team to pick up my mission A and respond as a whole, as one team. This did not happen. The difficulties of changing behaviour and autonomously starting to cooperate was bigger than expected and the team members would simply get lost in their old ways of interacting, not listening, arguing and wasting time. Clearly, the members of the leadership team were not yet in the 'here and now'. Individuals may think they can get away with this, especially when process cycle times are long. In such instances, people can believe in the luxury of avoiding the 'here and now' (as opposed to American football). This situation, however, is a time bomb and the organization will always pay dearly. Only later did I realize the ambiguity of the first point in my mission contract A: addressing the team by 'they' instead of 'it' is not asking for 'one voice'.

And still I was mistaken in thinking that the leadership team would swiftly come back with a mission contract B to express its needs and achieve coherence. In our contracting meetings, when reviewing the vision contract and mission contract A, speaking up was tough for the team and its discussions would be run by a small number of eloquent members; we really did not have a constructive dialogue between *one team* and the leader yet.

The biggest trouble was implementing point two of the mission contract A *on its own*. It was just not used to that kind of mutual activity without the leader, and the members needed autonomy in their relations to install autonomy in our relations. It was a sort of a stalemate. To avoid the automatic kick-in of my planning dynamic, I asked the leadership team to request assistance from the consultant in working on its cooperation contract and reviewing my mission contract A and to then issue a mission contract B, which they did. It was many weeks later when, with the help of the consultant and some inspired members, the leadership team finally did present its mission contract B:

- We need the leader to stand for the team during crisis (articulated support, leveraging, escalating)
- We would like to be trusted on our recommendations
- The leader communicates clearly, using simple, easily understood language
- The leader provides honest, authentic feedback
- The leader fosters team spirit and consults the team on incorporating new members
- We would like the leader to be proactive in recognizing the team's achievements

It was the first time the members expressed their needs explicitly as one team to the leader and an exciting point in the evolution of our human process. A group of people who had viewed performance at work as an individual

responsibility were now exchanging together on the requirements of our human relations. (Funny enough, I was of the
impression that I had been already doing all that.) In spite
of this terrific step, the differences in autonomy were still
apparent; members were not all on the same page. There
were signs of responsible action in the conversations during
our contracting, but not yet what one could easily identify
as interdependence. So, business kept its trod. One can keep
going in such a state and many organizations are doing this,
but only up to the next restructuring. An organization can
exist with regular projects, normal successes and problems
and hidden waste, but it will not embrace change sustainably and it will dawdle on its journey to excellence.

After another few months and in an external meeting,
the boat nearly capsized. As usual, we reviewed the vision
contract and objectives, which had evolved. We followed
with the review of the mission contract A, and I pushed for
point two, the cooperation contract. We knew it would be
a sensitive topic, but the leadership team's cooperation contract was the only way for us to have a chance to address the
waste in our processes and reach our ambitious objectives
in a sound and sustainable manner. After group works, participants reconvened for sharing the outcomes in plenum.
I sat on the sideline during one of the presentations when
suddenly pressure rose: faces turned red and voices started
to tremble, an unexpected outburst of emotions. The dis-
agreement, as it turned out, was strongly on using the hot
chair as the next step on the way to cooperation contract.

A very powerful exercise, the hot chair requires each participant to receive strokes from each member of the team
individually (Laugeri, 2015). Each member takes their turn

sitting in the middle of a semicircle, surrounded by their peers, and listens to each of their colleagues' testimony structured by three basic phrases:

• What I like about you is ...
• What surprises me about you is ...
• What I wish is ...

All comments are to be positive and encouraging, and the process needs to be closely supervised by a trained coach, for it can get out of hand and be misused for distributing penalties, a valid risk especially for first-time practitioners. It is the most crucial exercise for triggering the needs in human relations and developing autonomous cooperation within a team. (A preliminary exchange with a different purpose is the mirror chair: each team member will mirror to the rest his perception of his own experience, following the same sequence of expressions: What I appreciate, what is difficult, my request.)

Back in the meeting, the opinion leader, with eyes wide open and fists on the table, shared his disapproval of the hot chair: "Exchanging our feelings in a semicircle so all can hear is naïve, not professional and much too private. And, at any rate, this touchy-feely stuff is for kindergarten; we should rather bother about how we will achieve our targets. We have ambitious objectives and no time to lose." He was not alone. The meeting was close to rupture and it represented the best moment and opportunity for our coach to intervene. Once the audience had calmed down, she asked me if I was ok to leave the room. Now normally, as a leader, this is not what you would do, right? A good leader is expected to handle such situations and to motivate *his* team.

I said yes. Why? Because this was not *my* team; there was nothing I could do to help. The team needed to sort its cooperation out by itself and I would only be in the way.

When coming back two hours later the team, with tears still drying up, had reviewed their mission contract B and presented it to me with one voice. Everybody was in support and it was flabbergasting. The consultant had been working with the team on exchanging signs of recognition between the members and creating the first tender bonds for the strongly needed intimacy that had been missing in the team's former functioning. Shortly after we completed the first hot chair, the team issued its cooperation contract, which obviously I did not see as it is none of the leader's business. One could sense how the department heads felt supported by their colleagues; they were not all alone in their uncertainties.

Our contracted relationships addressed the waste of time in our interactions directly, in clear consciousness, not always with ease and pleasure, for our objectives were fierce, but when there was a smile it was genuine. We saved time *and* improved output. Pressure became manageable, confidence was up and trust was growing from day to day in the team's exchange. Our business threats and opportunities had not disappeared; however, addressing them and winning together as an organization was not a question anymore. We had been applying Six Sigma: launching yellow-belt, green-belt or black-belt projects, employing problem-solving tools, e.g., GSTD (go-see-think-do), DMAIC (define-measure-analyse-improve-control) and improving our business processes. Our knowledge documentation had been embedded in a magnificent competency and skills matrix for the entire expert community and, as team and leader, we were still standing every week in front of the Continuous Excellence Board presenting our key leading and lagging indicators. All this we did not change; it all continued, only now the leadership team cranked up one gear in performance by the one thing that did change: living our contracts in a human process with emerging change.

When installing the three contracts, teams and leaders thrive on:

- the rituals of expressing feelings and spirit and exchanging signs of recognition (e.g., meteo, mirror chair or hot chair)
- the rituals of contracting (vision contract, mission contract A and B and cooperation contract)
- the rituals of dialoguing constructively (scheduled time and offering space for exchanging missions A and B in 'ok-ness' and in the 'here and now' between the team and the leader and in cooperation in the team)

In such a constellation, it is the leadership team running the daily operations. The team relieves the leader of all the nitty-gritty decision-making and problem-solving for which, at any rate, he neither has the knowledge nor the needed information. As a leader, you do not need to know and master everything your direct reports do, a widely heard and accepted truth, which many companies acknowledge but unfortunately do not always translate into their management practices. Solicitations and questions from business partners, customers and suppliers concerning the operations are handled directly by the leadership team. Once the leader and team are in a continuous constructive dialogue, they can give the right focus on the long term with continuous updates of the vision contract and with the optimization of their strategic rush as response to the group's environment. It is more efficient and effective, but at the same time can become an issue for the leader if the rest of the organization does not follow the same process. The trouble is the external view of seeing the leader not intervene in the daily business or personally responding to external requests can induce the perception of *laissez faire* (letting things slip), of weak and insufficient leadership.

Vision and mission contracts evolve over time and become part of the daily organizational life. My next mission contract A which I presented was that the team:

1. Speaks up and says thank you
2. Installs a cooperation contract and cascades into the driver teams
3. Accelerates 'leadership through safety' for creating the constructive dialogue
4. Escalates failures immediately in the spirit of a learning team
5. Shares how the team wants to be rewarded
6. Installs a regular feedback process to the head of the centre

The leadership team responded right away with one voice and its mission contract B:

1. Support us in staying focused on our top priorities
2. Share important messages in a clear manner and in a relevant format (oral and written, back up system in place)
3. Clarify expectations when sharing important information: what is expected, by whom and when? FYI

(for your information), FA (for action) or FD (for decision, one person only)
4. Share strategic information from your primary teams of peers
5. Explain the 'why', when corporate/strategic/unexpected elements shift our tactic
6. Share failures in the spirit of walking the talk
7. Provide timely constructive feedback
8. Recognize our performance through specific positive feedback and a team event

These documents acted only as a reference for the contracting dialogues and for clarification of the desired human relations, nothing else.

We soon set up a global R+D for the product group using the three contracts. We grouped the existing responsibilities and activities in the centres in Europe, North America and Asia under one leadership. First, we paved the way for a cooperation contract between peers, a team of R+D centre heads spread around the globe and staff leads at the head office. In the beginning, we invested into meetings face to face, establishing our human process and using the emerging change model. Once we were on an 'ok-base', we could regularly go straight to the point with no hidden agendas. Pretty soon we communicated solely by our visual digital network until the completion of our objectives. We issued the vision contract and as the leader of this new R+D organization, I presented the mission contract A to the new decentralized leadership team. Each member had his vision and mission contracts with his team spread over three continents. The new leadership team presented its mission B to me without delay; it had been built on the existing cooperation contracts; they acted as accelerators. Some members of the leadership team, e.g., the head of human resources, capitalized on their knowledge and experience of applying the three contracts and acted as coaches for further implementation in the new organization.

We were in coherence with the objectives because we could continuously address our conflicts openly and constructively in our contracting space and in spite of the substantial personal changes, including cost reduction, we could ensure proactive responses to the needs of the people involved in the change. In our dialogues, some of a critical nature concerning capital investments and divestments, we assured respect of the different opinions and decision with consensus; in the course of installing the new structures, we hit the ground running and one could see coherence grow through the new organization. Output increased while the different parts of the organization cooperated fast and efficiently. It all resulted in the delivery of a series of significant innovations for the Asian and European markets and in the course of the following year, top and bottom lines in the business advanced above expectations. Additionally, brand values experienced substantial growth in an increasingly competitive environment and the teams supporting the business were internally recognized and rewarded.

10

INSTALLING A HUMAN PROCESS WITH EMERGING CHANGE IN THE ORGANIZATION

"When adjustments in human relationships are done by default, satisfying our relational needs in the agreed rituals is prioritized over the completion of the agreed tasks."

Madeleine Laugeri

Doing good must start small. Emerging change, as in these examples, was launched in a segment and then spread to the rest of organization. Contracts were not simultaneously applied and this is absolutely fine. Installing emerging change means initiating the three contracts in a fractal way, starting anywhere. Figure 7 shows simplified structure diagrams of teams with their leaders. Each outer circle represents the major external boundary of a team, the inner circle the major internal boundary. The minor internal boundaries between team members (TM) are intentionally omitted in the diagram for simplification. The teams are in a hierarchical relationship and a team member (TM) of one team can be the leader (L) of another, depicted by line (a): we are wearing different hats at different times and for different purposes. This can be the case for all team members; however, to keep a clear image in the diagram, only a small number of lines (a) are drawn. The team with its leader is the fractal with optimally 7 to 10 and a maximum of 12 to 15 group members and each fractal follows the model of emerging change. The vision contract is applied across the major external boundary and the leader ensures alignment with the vision contracts of the adjacent teams. The mission contracts A and B are exchanged in a constructive dialogue between leader and the team as one entity across the major internal boundary of each fractal, and each team creates its cooperation contract between peers. This way, every leader works on the vision and mission contracts with the reporting team and is at the same time part of a cooperation contract with his peers as a team member (TM). This cooperation contract is again the basis for a mission contract B responding to the mission contract A of the next level in the hierarchy. By expansion across the whole organization, lines (c), lasting coherence between the needs at any end and the objectives from the top of an organization is achieved. One can imagine a network of the three contracts between all the different leaders and their corresponding teams independently of size, status and position.

Line (b) in the diagram shows how an individual can be a team member (TM) of two separate teams; for example, when working on multiple projects. Changing teams easily and belonging to more than one project will make sense to people as the very same human process with emerging change is applied independently of the objectives and the mission content of any group the individuals adhere to. By applying the three contracts in a fractal manner, the organization mirrors the federal structure and the interaction in groups in Switzerland's communities, its states (cantons) and the confederation. Such an organization benefits continuously from greater flexibility, optimal costs and higher performance. Success is built on maintaining consistently and permanently high-performing human relations.

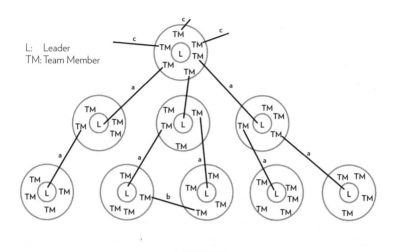

FIGURE 7

INSTALLING EMERGING CHANGE IN AN ORGANIZATION

Emerging change answers to the new human challenges and requirements of our evolving work environment. We have seen powerful management tools and methods successfully applied in the past, but hitting a wall today when it comes to improving people-centred management. Behaviour-based management systems, such as for occupational health and safety, produce excellent results in their field. However, as effective as they are, I believe they have come to their limits. We should evolve from prioritizing people-centred management at the level of individual employees to seeking answers to future business expectations, e.g., how groups of people and teams can develop, strive for excellence and succeed in an organization. Results can take a quantum leap when organizations move from individual autonomy to team autonomy and cooperation, thanks to the opportunity of emergence; it is for sports, politics and business alike.

When it comes to relationships on the job, the younger generations entering work life today, sometimes referred to as Millennials and Generations Y and Z, have their own expectations. Their integration into the digital world and their understanding of its evolution is special: as kids, teenagers or students, they are fully immersed and this definitely influences the workplace dynamics arising ahead of us. Young professionals are wishing for more thoughtful relations between all workers and employers, and they are not afraid to express their needs and take the consequences if those are not responded to. Their connectedness in their daily lives calls for openness to input from anywhere and everyone in real time, in the 'here and now', which then should result in immediate action. Hierarchy is not fundamentally questioned, but of different importance. In their minds, the boss exists first of all for their support and for being ready to help on request so they can take work matters in their own hands. This is undoubtedly a situation requiring effective two-way communication between leader and team and, in anticipation, leaders may have to envisage changing their style. We should be aware of what we are facing; just telling the newcomers to wait, listen and do their jobs will not suffice anymore.

More than ever, the workforce of the future is looking for flexibility in their tasks, personal development and professional fulfillment. Now, this does not sound unfamiliar and one can say it has been important to any conscientious employee for a long time. The coming generation's dreams and wishes are likely not so different from those of any young people before; definitely they arise from our human nature, for we all would like to be recognized and nobody really wants to be singled out or patronized. The digital revolution, however, has evoked the conditions and opportunities for getting used to creating one's own type of environment with a minimal amount of effort. People today are globally connected already at a very young age and this has changed their experiences, horizons and expectations irreversibly. Working not only in the office but from home or far places is a common reality today. How will organizations respond to other future demands of fulfilment at work, of taking responsibilities and of living equally at all levels? I believe the real challenge for organizations will not be the cooperation contract. The new generations are ready; they are expecting cohesion. The big development will be in the vision and mission contracts. How will we ensure cohesion *and* coherence in this new environment? It cannot be the exception anymore for leaders to dialogue with teams in a constructive way, and all teams will want to cooperate in full autonomy. Vision and mission will be modulated and expanded between peers, not only through the hierarchy, and some of what we call leadership responsibilities today will be handled by teams.

Figure 8 shows the structure diagrams of two teams. In the one on the right, the team does not have a single leader anymore. Such a case can imply a whole array of possible contracting dynamics for establishing coherence. For starters, one can imagine the team members (TM) in the inner circle of the diagram to the right, issuing and living their cooperation contract. These three leaders coming from the leadership team, in figure 8 on p.170, cover a wider area of activities and responsibilities than one leader alone would, which offers bigger and better opportunities for the direct reports (tm) to emerge and improve performance. This team of direct reports (tm) establishes its cooperation contract and partly or fully takes over the vision contract at the major external boundary (outer circle). Both parties (TM and tm) will negotiate and dialogue as teams in their mission contract A and B for covering their needs across the major internal boundary. The development of emergence in such a structure leads to increased flexibility, quicker and more direct response to surrounding forces and ensures simultaneous fulfilment of the necessities and the requirements of the people in different parts of the organization. Isn't it what we all are looking for?

A European business operating with teams as leaders demonstrates how the structure of the organization will be adapted through emerging change. The three members of the European operation's leadership team, as shown in the structure diagram of Figure 8, responsible for the functions engineering, quality and logistics (TM), install a multifunctional team consisting of their direct reports (tm). Its mission is to cooperate in supporting the improvements of production as a single point of contact for all of the European factories. The functional heads of the technical leadership team (TM) install a cooperation contract, while one representative passes on its mission contract A with one voice to the team of direct reports (tm). The latter installs its cooperation contract and emerges in a constructive dialogue through its mission contract B with the aim of eliminating duplications between functions and improving performance in its activities. It also responds, in autonomous cooperation, directly to the requirements of its environment and issues the vision contract with the factories, the business and other stakeholders. Streamlining of the activities and alignment of the supporting structures with the requirements of production are discussed and agreed on through the contracts. This can consequently lead to combining responsibilities at the functional heads' level (TM) and reduction of the number of leaders. The structure of the organization is adapted, while at the same time the benefits of the synergies and the reduction of duplications in the support of the factories lead to increased efficiency.

The Federal Council of Switzerland is the most extensive application of team leadership and of autonomous cooperation fostering emergence, at least of which 1 am aware. The highest level of power of a country of eight million inhabitants represents four of the five largest political parties and close to 70% of the voting population after the elections in October 2019; its cooperation is perceived as the symbol of concordance for the nation and from its cooperation contract emerges the mutual responses to the strategic elements of its activities for reaching the country's objectives. The Federal Council derives, out of this sharing of their activities, its vision contract; its mission contracts are exchanged in dialogue with parliament, in the house of representatives and the senate. These principles flow into the decentralized structure of the confederation, and they persist and outlive the changing composition of the councils. It is the Swiss way of changing sustainably, the heartbeat of excellence, which has shaped and moulded the country and stamped freedom and prosperity on its society.

L: Leader
TM/tm: Team Member

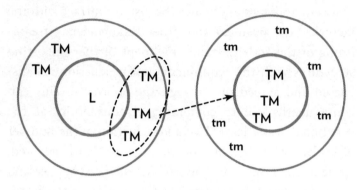

FIGURE 8

TEAM LEADERSHIP WITH EMERGING CHANGE

In the same manner, teams in business – starting with any leadership team – working in a human process with emerging change will continue to live their cooperation contracts despite personnel changes in team compositions or leadership positions. Every fractal can continue emerging on its own. Interdependency is not only in but also among fractals through the cooperation contracts of the leaders, and once the contracts are adopted and the rituals established, the organization may enter into a virtuous circle where the resulting dynamics guarantee coherence over time. A virtuous circle for continuous improvement powered by a human process with emerging change is pivotal in the journey to excellence of an organization.

This journey may lead to a virtuous circle; it starts with an initial alignment in the organization, meaning the objectives and the people's performance are coherent. It implies that the needs of all workers are met to achieve the organizational targets. This is shown in Step 1 of Figure 9. Eric Berne says that in a group of people, all will develop their talents and preferences to the best of their interests. Following the law of increasing entropy, the organization will face divergence of interests and needs, eroding the existing coherence, unless the leaders and the teams spend the required energy to make sure their needs stay aligned with the evolving objectives. Continuously ensuring this coherence demands conscious intervention. 'Managing coherence' (Step 2 of Figure 9) is facilitated by a human process with emerging change, where leaders and teams interact in the frame of the three contracts and their constructive dialogue, and they adjust expectations before coherence is at stake. It is the secret of the Swiss way of changing sustainably. In such a context, the personal and professional development of the people are addressed, motivational levels increase and performance of the organization improves (Step 3) and consequently, new targets and standards are set, to which each fractal aligns again (Step 1). This will go as far as leading to the simplification of an organization's structure, for in this virtuous circle structure is continuously adapted to the needs of the evolving organization.

One might think of the virtuous circle as an esoteric adventure. It is not. It includes a constant exchange of different opinions in a constructive dialogue, tough decisions, efficiency in resources, new structures and people having to change significantly; however, it all happens by respecting the people in the fractal of team and leader throughout the organization. The European business organization, as in the example above, has been recognized for consistently and continuously producing excellent results. For the last five years in a row, at the end of the year all eyes are on the operations, which again have outperformed their targets. When questioned how this is possible, the head of operations answers: "Vision, mission and cooperation contracts … but nobody believes me."

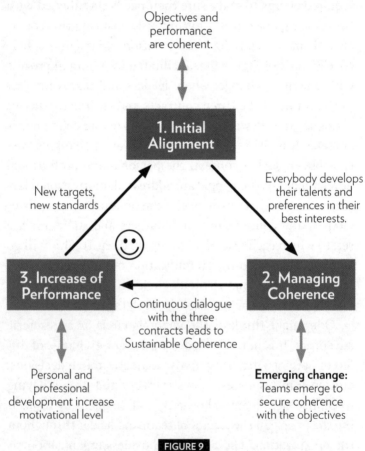

FIGURE 9

THE VIRTUOUS CIRCLE WITH EMERGING CHANGE

Virtuous circles are plentiful in management models. What is unique in this model to what I have seen in the past is that it eliminates the gap of what leaders expect and what teams need *in anticipation*, using the powerful tool of the three contracts. This single fact makes an enormous difference to the survival of a company and for its journey to excellence. Instead of costly top-down restructuring, change becomes a sustainable process. Changing sustainably is an evolutionary process, and is the very heartbeat of excellence, where new results are built on former ones and where there is unlimited opportunity for unthinkable innovations and improvements to emerge.

Therefore, the hypothesis stands that the new paradigm shift in the organizational world of today and tomorrow is emergence. We have missed a structured, brief intervention specific to the team for generating and breeding emergence and allowing the team to federate and ensure adequate exchange of strategic information and requests related to the group's activity. Here it is: a human process with emerging change and its three contracts. Potential applications of emerging change are limitless ever since. All groups have three boundaries in their human interactions, and the human contracts can be observed even if their existence is not recognized and formalized by the group. From kindergarten to university, in any type of business and surely in the context of the family, the unconscious effects of the group boundaries on people's feelings and behaviours can be powerfully transformed with the help of the three contracts. The model of emerging change can sound complicated and perhaps be judged as overkill at first glance. Mission A and B, vision and cooperation contracts are guiding terminologies for what human beings would consider normal and common sense. Emerging change does not reinvent; it merely ensures cohesion and coherence in the structure for changing sustainably in our organizational environment. It is hard to explain and has to be experienced in order to understand its profound effect on our lives, which then renders it completely evident.

Our world is exhibiting the urgent need for changing sustainably, the Swiss way, and the shift to emergence must not stop at the frontiers of business organizations. People-centred management ensuring coherence should be the first priority in any organization. However, instead of gaining, we get the impression we are losing coherence in the national and international political, economic and social constructs of the present day. It seems autocracies, nationalism and even despotism are increasing around our globe, in contrast to what we would want to believe or wish for. When contemplating the global political landscapes, we cannot deny the difficulties of spotting functioning direct democracies; this is a pity, as they could very well act as the nurseries for emergence and coherence to germinate, and for the process of changing sustainably, the Swiss way, to grow and flourish. Democracies should offer the moral frame, the control mechanisms and the autonomous cooperation for emergence to take a foothold in our societies. If autonomous cooperation is not in place, agitation and polarization is guaranteed. They fill the void. When political heavyweights exhibit indifference to our human moral frame and dish out hatred, lies or fake news, they polarize. It is the big drawback of oppositional governments, democratic or not. Many leaders and parties tend to overlook the universal, unbeatable long-term benefits of autonomous cooperation resulting from emergence and the fact of having different opinions in a group of people should add value and not be a reason for prosecution.

If there is the demand for speeding up our cultural evolution, not by chance but through conscious efforts and for establishing the urgently needed coherence in our societies, then emerging change is our response.

CONCLUSION

Emerging change responds to the desire to aspire to a new era of people-centred management. Emerging change mobilizes people's untapped potential, involving all by creating autonomous cooperation and interdependency in teams and forms the leadership style of the future. Both are of undeniable interest to any organization. The example of American football teams is convincing evidence of how autonomy, cooperation and interdependency deliver top performance founded on trust and reliance without hesitation. They constitute the prime conditions for emergence to flourish, conditions which are and have been the essential ingredients for the success of a team of professionals, from the hunters of prehistoric times who dared not fail in making their catch to any high-performing team in today's businesses.

Appreciation of our emotions in reasoning and decision-making is fundamental in high-performing human relations; we all need to accept and strive on conscious and unconscious knowledge and expertise transmitted by our feelings. In such an environment, innovations emerge and the process of change becomes sustainable, analogous to our biological and homologous to our cultural evolutionary development, in a process of changing sustainably. The rules of the game and of the universe decide what perishes, what stays and for how long. In the realm of physics, chemistry or even biology, this is quite obvious, but we still lack awareness of the importance of this process for our cultural evolution.

Fostering emergence in people-centred management should be high priority in any organization. Switzerland, with its direct democracy, federal structure and executive management by teams (councils), is a prime example of the power of emergence on the journey to excellence. An organization keeps changing sustainably – the Swiss way – if change is permitted to emerge. This is a journey we all must embark on if we want to find the very heartbeat of excellence. It will not only change our organizations, I believe, but it has the power to change our lives.

BIBLIOGRAPHY

Anderson, P.W. (1972). "More is Different." *Science*, New Series, Vol 177, No. 404; pp.393–396.

The Arbinger Institute (2009). *Leadership and Self-Deception: Getting Out of the Box*. London/New York: Berrett-Koehler Publishers.

Atmani, M. (2018). "Le Grand Bluff du travail «à la cool»". *PME Magazine*, August 9, pp. 36-40.

Bergier, J. F. (1988). *Wilhelm Tell*. München: List Verlag.

Berne, E. (1963). *Structure and Dynamics of Organizations and Groups*. Ballantine Books.

Damasio, A.R. (2010). *Descartes' Irrtum*. Berlin: List Taschenbuch.

Esslinger, H. (2012). *Design Forward*. Stuttgart: Arnoldsche Art Publishers.

Fretwell, P. & Kiland, T.B. (2013). *Lessons from the Hanoi Hilton*. Annapolis: Naval Institute Press.

Frey, B. & Osterloh, M. (2018). "Paradoxie der digitalen Welt." Gastkommentar, *Neue Zürcher Zeitung*, 16 January.

Forbes. (2019). "The World's Most Valuable Brands: 2019 ranking." https://www.forbes.com/powerful-brands/list/#tab:rank

Fulghum, R. (1990). *All I Really Need to Know I Learned in Kindergarten*. New York: Villard Books.

Gesundheitsförderung Schweiz (2018). "Job-Stress-Index 2016." https://gesundheitsfoerderung.ch/ueber-uns/medien/ medienmitteilungen/artikel/job-stress-index-2018-jede-vierteerwerbstaetige-person-hat-stress.html

Hagel, J., Brown, J.S., Wooll, M., & de Maar, A. (2016). *2016 Shift Index.* Deloitte Insights. https://www2.deloitte.com/us/en/insights/ multimedia/infographics/shift-index.html

Handy, C. (1994). *The Empty Raincoat.* London: Hutchinson.

Harshak, A., Aguirre, D., & Brown, A. (2010). *Making Change Happen, and Making It Stick: Delivering Sustainable Organizational Change.* Strategy & (formerly Booz & Company).

Herman, E. (2012). "Harry F. Harlow, Monkey Love Experiments." The Adoption History Project. https://pages.uoregon.edu/ adoption/studies/HarlowMLE.htm

Kaltenecker, S. (2015). *Leading Self-Organizing Teams.* C4Media.

Kaplan, P. (2018). "Derek Barnett recovers fumble to help Philadelphia Eagles win Super Bowl." *Knox news* (USA Today Network), February 5. https://eu.knoxnews.com/story/sports/college/university-of-tennessee/football/2018/02/04/derek-barnett-recovers-fumble-help-philadelphia-eagles-win-super-bowl/305950002/

Katzenbach, J.R. & Smith, D.K. (2005). *The Wisdom of Teams: Creating the High-Performance Organization.* London: McGraw-Hill.

Laugeri, M. (2015). *Les clés du dialogue hiérarchique.* Paris: InterEditions.

Laugeri, M. (2018). "Emerging Change, a New Transactional Analysis Frame for Effective Dialogue at Work." Article submitted to the *Transactional Analysis Journal.*

Lorenz, K. (1980). *Die Rückseite des Spiegels.* (4th edition.) München: Deutscher Taschenbuch Verlag.

Maissen, T. (2015). *Schweizer Heldengeschichten.* Baden: Hier und Jetzt, Verlag für Kultur und Geschichte.

Marquet, L.D. (2015). *Turn the Ship Around.* Portfolio Penguin.

McChrystal, S. (2015). *Team of Teams.* Penguin Books.

Ono, T. (2013). *Das Toyota-Produktions-System*. Frankfurt/New York: Campus Verlag.

Pellerin, G. (1994). "Diagnostic rapide des organisations." *Actualité en Analyse Transactionelle*, No. 71.

Peters, T.J. & Austin, N.K. (1985). *A Passion for Excellence*. New York: Warner Books Edition.

Peters, T.J. & Waterman, R.H. (2004). *In Search of Excellence*. New York: Harper Collins.

QS Top Universities (2019). "QS World University Rankings by Subject 2019: Engineering and Technology." https://www.topuniversities.com/university-rankings/university-subject-rankings/2019/engineering.

Raelin, J.A. (2011). "From Leadership-as-Practice to Leaderful Practice." *Leadership*, Vol 7, No. 2, SAGE Publications.

Smith, A. (2000). *The Theory of Moral Sentiments*. Prometheus Books.

Steiner, C. (2009). *The Heart of the Matter*. TA Press.

Stewart, L. (2009). "Relational Needs." Lindsay Stewart M.S.W., R.C.S.W.: Registered Clinical Social Worker. http://www.lindsaystewart-psychotherapy.com/relational-needs/. 19 June.

Tomasello, M. (2008). "Origins of Human Cooperation." The Tanner Lectures on Human Values, delivered at Stanford University, October 29-31.

Tuckman, B.W. (1965). "Developmental sequence in small groups." *Psychological Bulletin*, Vol 63, No. 6; June pp.384-399.

Ubha, R. & Macfarlane, C. (2019). *"Roger Federer's tears for former coach: 'Never broke down like this'."* CNN Sports, January 8. https://edition.cnn.com/2019/01/07/tennis/federer-carter-emotion-tennis-spt-intl/index.html

Van Poejle, S. (1994). "Contracting for Organizational Change." Volume of selected articles, *Maastricht*.

Villiger, K. (2015). *Demokratie und konzeptionelles Denken*. Zürich: Verlag Neue Zürcher Zeitung.

ACKNOWLEDGMENTS

My sincere thanks and deep gratitude go to:

The many great people that are part of the stories and whom I had the privilege and the joy to meet and work with.

Detlef, our dear friend, a natural in applying the three contracts and a remarkable leader.

Madeleine who has inspired and supported me over the years.

Olivier Robin for his experience and opinions offered during our dinners and his tenacity in the support of the Emerging Change Model.

Olivier Champion and his insight into how American football teams work.

Regine and Alois, fellow Young Leaders, for investing in reading through my manuscript and sharing their insights.

Stefan for caring and for his visionary thinking in our discussions and constructive debates over the last years.

Urs, our truthful friend who interviews federal councillors while cross country skiing.

My family whose input and recommendations are part of this book.